THE WHICH? computer

troubleshooter

About the author

Robin Davies, once a music teacher, first became involved with computers in the early 1980s. Hooked by the Internet before the advent of the Worldwide Web, he's worked in PC support, local government IT management and as a freelance trainer. He now lives in Wales, doing contract IT support work, and also runs a website-hosting-and-development business with his son.

THE WHICH? computer
troubleshooter

ROBIN DAVIES

BOOKS

CONSUMERS' ASSOCIATION

CONTENTS

INTRODUCTION

Since the first IBM PC went on sale in 1981, a PC's power has doubled almost every two years. Prices of hardware have fallen rapidly. What cost £1,000 in 2000 costs £599 or less now (January 2002), and a buyer's choice is immense. Colour printing is the norm. Complex and powerful software is readily available, as are high-speed action games. You can buy the latest movies on DVD and play them at home. TV programmes can be watched on-screen and recorded to your PC's hard disk.

The most challenging and exciting development in recent years is undoubtedly the rise of the Internet. Even in the early 1990s it was the domain of the few, but nearly everyone who buys a new PC now will connect to the Internet, and almost 40 per cent of the population of the UK now has access. Every school – even the smallest rural ones – in the UK can go online. There are public access points in every library, never mind Internet cafés and access from work. This book will offer you guidance in accessing the Internet safely and some tips on dealing with the most common issues and problems.

The Which? Computer Troubleshooter aims to help solve the problems and answer the questions you may have in the course of using a PC. No technical knowledge on the part of the reader has been assumed and the book takes care to set the scene for each topic before launching into troubleshooting mode.

The book offers simple explanations, useful tips and guidelines for more advanced troubleshooting. It deciphers computer jargon and provides instructions for configuring software and hardware. You will find advice on repairing and upgrading your PC. The glossary at the end of the book explains the most common acronyms and computer jargon.

This book focuses on the most recent version of Windows – XP – but also provides useful support for users of the older versions (Windows 98, ME and 2000). Windows 95 became officially obsolete in November 2001.

What this book is not is a substitute for the user manuals that come with some PCs. In reality, few manufacturers supply extensive documentation, and what is provided is often too technical and limited in scope. It is always worth remembering that Windows itself, in all versions, comes with extensive Help files – as do all commercial Windows programs.

Of all the ways to learn about computers, the best is through guided trial and error. Like good car mechanics, electricians, plumbers and carpenters, many so-called computer experts are often self-taught. They have got to grips with the basic principles and have then experimented with hardware and software to solve problems – just as you can.

With the help of *The Which? Computer Troubleshooter* and, no doubt, a little trial and error, we hope that you will soon be in a similar position.

Buying a scanner

Scanners can now be bought for less than £40. These are rather slow, scan at lower resolution than more expensive devices and normally connect via the parallel port. If you also have a parallel port printer, that has to be connected to the scanner, and both machines need to be on for printing to work. Better scanners – costing about £100 – connect via the USB or SCSI port.

The combination of constantly falling PC prices and seemingly ever-increasing technological power makes it hard for a buyer to make the right choice of computer at the right time. There are two golden rules. First, decide what you want to do with a PC and, second, stick to your budget.

WHAT DO YOU WANT TO DO WITH YOUR PC?

| **Mostly fast, arcade-like action games** | Consoles such as Playstation, N64, Dreamcast and Microsoft's Xbox offer a comparatively cheap alternative to a PC. | If you are set on a PC, you need a fast graphics card (at least 32Mb RAM) and at least 256Mb of system RAM. |

Basic PC

You do not need a top-of-the-range PC for word-processing and Internet access. Cheap PCs based on Intel Celeron or AMD Duron processors and 64Mb RAM cope well with those tasks. Make sure you buy one with a modem and look around for deals that include a printer. Many cheap PCs comes with packages like Microsoft's Works Suite (which includes Word 2000 or 2002), which is adequate for most users. Alternatives are Lotus SmartSuite and Star Office. Keep your eye on computer-magazine-cover CDs as you will regularly find out-of-date packages available free.

Power bracket

This is the expensive end of the market, aimed perhaps at someone looking to do serious creative work with graphics, video or music. With fast AMD or Intel processors and a minimum of 256Mb RAM, these top-end PCs should come with a minimum hard disk size of 40Gb, plus the usual DVD & CD/R-W drives. Naturally, it will have a big monitor – at least 19 inch – and surround-sound speaker systems. An inkjet printer that delivers photographic-quality output and a flatbed scanner are essential too. Powerful PCs in this bracket will also be more than able to meet the 'edutainment' needs of a family. You should look for good-value bundles offering all the above, along with options for up to three years' warranty.

Family PC

This is for anyone who is not on a tight budget and is looking for a multi-purpose PC capable of handling the education and entertainment needs of a family. It is likely to have a fast AMD Athlon or Intel P4 processor, lots of RAM, a DVD drive (for watching films), good graphics and soundcards, a 17-inch monitor and probably a printer and/or scanner in the package. A modem is a must and a CD/R-W drive may be an essential upgrade, if not part of the package. Some packages in this market might include a digital camera as an alternative to a scanner or as a low-cost upgrade. Software is likely to be Windows XP (Home Edition), Microsoft Works Suite or even Office Standard. Software and driver CDs and manuals should be matched by a decent warranty of two years with the first year onsite.

Users should remember that virtually all PCs can be upgraded and this book will offer you help and guidance in this area in later sections.

Buying second-hand PCs and printers

With prices of hardware, even at the basic level, dropping constantly, buying second-hand is not that attractive. This is certainly true of printers. Basic colour inkjet printers can be bought new for as little as £60. In modern inkjet printers, the technology is in the printing heads – which is why buying a black cartridge and a colour cartridge at the same time can cost over £30. It is increasingly difficult to buy cartridges for really old inkjet printers and they simply cannot produce the quality of output of a modern colour inkjet (see 'Choosing a colour printer', below).

Try to pay by cheque or credit card as this provides a paper trail in case the machine was stolen: you can at least prove you bought it from the seller.

PCs bought second-hand can still be worth considering, but check the following.

• If you buy one from a shop, it should come with a 90-day warranty and a detailed written specification of the PC. You are covered by the Sale of Goods Act if the PC you buy does not match the written specification.
• There is little point in buying a PC that is not at least a Pentium P166.
• Avoid PCs that do not have Windows already installed and working properly.
• Try to get a machine that runs at least Windows 98 SE; if you want to upgrade to Windows XP, you will need at least a Pentium II as specified in the sidebar.
• Always test a machine before you buy. This includes the floppy drive, CD-ROM and display. It is worth taking a knowledgeable friend along with you.

CHOOSING A COLOUR PRINTER

Most home users go a for a colour inkjet printer. Today's inkjets are capable of astonishingly high resolution printing of photographic quality (especially on photographic paper) at prices unheard of only a few years ago. Black and white printing can easily be of 'laser' quality. Buying a really good inkjet can cost less than £150; an adequate one can cost as little as £60. However, inkjets can be expensive to run. All the technology is now in the cartridge, with the mechanism just acting as a means of moving the print head across the paper. That is why branded cartridges can cost upwards of £20. Do not buy an inkjet with only one cartridge. It is essential to buy inkjets with separate black and colour cartridges.

Laser printers come into their own for faster, cheaper black and white printing. They cost more to buy than inkjets, but even so, a basic laser printer can be bought for less than £190. Running costs are much less than for a colour inkjet, at about a third of the cost per page. Colour lasers are still probably too expensive for the casual home user. The cheapest cost at least £2,000 and running costs are much higher.

Integrated units that combine colour inkjet printing, scanning and copying in one desktop unit are growing in popularity. Apart from saving space, they can carry out copying functions without the PC being switched on. Some also act as fax machines.

Laptops

Although much more expensive than a comparable desktop PC (around 80 per cent more), they are great if you travel often and need a PC for work. Upgrades are more expensive, as are repairs. Warranties almost always require sending the laptop away. Check the price of extended warranties carefully.

Which version of Windows?

Windows XP, which was released on 25 October 2001, needs a decent processor (at least a 600MHz+ Intel Celeron or AMD Duron), a minimum of 128Mb RAM and an adequate hard disk (10Gb at least). Any specification higher than that should be fine for XP. Second-hand PCs can easily run Windows 95, 98 or ME. Of those, avoid Windows 95 – it is obsolete, slow and prone to bugs.

WARRANTIES

PC warranties have a language of their own. The jargon can be almost impenetrable and although after-sales service is a vital part of the purchase it can be difficult to know what you're getting. The three kinds of warranty are:

- 'onsite': the best type to have, because if there is a problem a computer engineer will visit your home or office to sort it out
- 'collect and return' (C&R), the next best type, under which the PC manufacturer will send a courier to collect the PC from you, then sort out the problem on its own premises. There is no charge for this — just the inconvenience of having to stay in twice for couriers
- 'return to base' (RTB): this has many similarities to C&R in that the PC must go back to the manufacturer for repair, but under this arrangement you must arrange and pay for the carriage.

As well as knowing what type of warranty you have, you should find out whether repairs are carried out within a guaranteed time period. Most onsite warranties pledge to have an engineer by your side the next working day (sometimes subject to the initial call being logged before a particular time), with faster service available for a price. If the PC has to go back for repair, most companies will endeavour to return it to you within a week or a fortnight. Including travelling time for the machine, this is reasonable. Although even the most respectable manufacturers may only guarantee a 28-day turnround time, this is simply to cover their backs. Any company which mutters about how long a repair will take and warns of typical turnrounds of four or six weeks is probably trying to play on your fears to sell you an extended warranty.

Whether it is worth paying more for onsite cover is up to you. Assuming a reasonably quick turnround, a return-to-base warranty is adequate for home users. All onsite cover gives you is convenience, but if you are running a business, onsite maintenance may be essential. Extending the standard one-year warranty given by the PC manufacturer to cover, say, three years' onsite cover should not cost much more than £100—£150; if you want a guaranteed response within a shorter period, such as four hours, it will be more expensive.

One thing to watch out for is having to call a helpline. Check the call charge rates, as some suppliers use premium-rate numbers costing up to £1 per minute. Advertisements and information sheets should state clearly what the calls will cost. Even local call rates (0845) or national rates (0870) can add up if you are in a queue for 20 minutes – especially during the day. Note that software bought with your PC, such as Windows and Microsoft Office, may be supported only by the manufacturer of the machine. Microsoft staff have been known to be unwilling to talk to end-users. If you can still connect to the Internet, the supplier's website may prove helpful and you can often send emails and receive effective help from support staff.

What warranties cover

A warranty will normally cover only actual mechanical faults. If the problem you are experiencing is caused by software configuration the PC manufacturer is unlikely to offer any help; it may instead redirect you to the software manufacturer's support line.

Buying system components from various suppliers often causes manufacturers to pass the responsibility for warranties to the others, which is a good reason for sticking to a single supplier. A single supplier is also more cost-effective if you need an extended or comprehensive warranty package.

Purchase protection

The first worry when buying a PC by mail order is whether it will arrive at all: it has been known for computer-assembly companies to take a stack of orders, cash the cheques and then vanish with the money.

Fortunately, these cases are rare, though this is small comfort if you are unfortunate enough to be caught. However, protecting yourself is relatively easy. Most important is to buy from a reputable company. Magazine reviews can help here: companies which make a consistently good showing over a period of months are well worth shortlisting.

If possible, pay by credit card. The Consumer Credit Act ensures that the card issuer is jointly liable for any private purchase between £100 and £30,000: if your computer does not arrive, you will get your money back. In theory, this also makes the card issuer liable for any warranty problems that arise, though in practice you will find this more helpful in applying pressure to the manufacturer than in making it accept responsibility.

Note that this protection does not apply to credit cards first issued before 1971, to debit cards (e.g. Switch or Delta), to charge cards such as American Express, or to company purchases.

Although buying from a magazine advertisement carrying the Mail Order Protection Scheme logo may seem safe, do not rely on this. It is hedged with restrictions – for instance, your purchase may have to have been the exact model advertised in the magazine – and a strict cash limit ensures that few people can be recompensed in respect of any one advertiser.

Extended warranties

Be wary of extended warranties, which are often aggressively sold, over-priced, and unclear about what they offer.

Assuming that the standard warranty covers one year's onsite maintenance followed by another two years of return-to-base cover, you should expect an extension to three years' onsite to cost about £100. You may pay more if the standard warranty offers less in the first place. If you feel you are being given the 'hard sell', especially if the small print includes dire warnings about the shortcomings of the standard warranty, steer clear. The odds are that the salesperson stands to earn a handsome commission if you sign up.

One of the main advantages of a desktop PC is its flexibility. The variety of software available is huge, and ranges from small programs, which improve the functioning of a PC, to large and complex software suites of programs such as Microsoft Office. Plenty of free or cheap programs are available, many offered as 'shareware' (try before buying). One thing is certain: you will find something for every need and everybody.

Throughout this guide you will find examples of menus and configuration screens taken from Windows XP, which was released in October 2001. Windows 98, ME (Millennium Edition) and Windows 2000 are also covered where there are significant differences. Windows 95 became obsolete in November 2001.

Windows 98 and ME have much in common because they share the same programming code base. Windows NT, 2000 and XP share a different and much more reliable code base. Windows XP is designed to replace all earlier versions of Windows – both at home and at work – and looks very different. Its key partner program – Office XP – will not run on Windows 95 at all.

Most new PCs from September 2000 to November 2001 came with Windows ME and most new PCs sold from October 2001 have had Windows XP installed. If you are thinking of buying a PC or have bought one recently, this book is designed to help you. Those readers still using Windows 98 and ME will find much to help them.

This chapter is designed to familiarise new users with the basic hardware and software elements of a modern desktop PC running with the Windows operating system. Please note that different PC manufacturers may customise Windows with different colour schemes, settings and supplementary programs. As the number of possible variations is huge, we have stuck to the most common settings as our basis for explanations and troubleshooting.

Before you take the lid off your PC, it is essential that you learn about the basic menus and settings covered in this chapter. However, remember that if you do make a mistake you are unlikely to damage your PC permanently. Windows XP is particularly designed to help you restore a system after accidentally deleting key files. Making mistakes can be the best way to learn!

INTRODUCING YOUR PC

1 | Introducing your PC

THE PERSONAL COMPUTER

Cables and sockets

When a PC is being set up, usually the cables will fit in only one way. On modern PCs, the keyboard and mouse connectors are exactly the same size and shape, so suppliers normally either colour-code the plugs and sockets or label them. If you do plug them in the wrong way, you will get an explicit error message.

For a personal computer (PC) to work it needs hardware and software. Hardware consists primarily of the screen, the system unit (main box), the keyboard and the mouse. Software comprises programs such as word-processing packages, databases and games. To operate both hardware and software you need to have an operating system — the most common of these is Windows. This section introduces you to the main parts of your computer system.

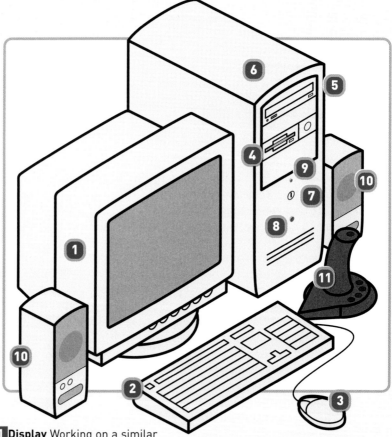

Warning!

As a safety precaution, you should never plug in or remove peripherals while the system is switched on. The exception to this rule is USB (see section 1.9), which is specifically designed for plugging in while the PC is still on (often referred to as 'hot swapping').

1 Display Working on a similar principle to a television, the computer screen (also called the monitor or visual display unit) shows what the computer is doing.

2 Keyboard A PC keyboard has between 102 and 117 keys normally arranged in a similar way to a typewriter. It allows you to enter text and has special keys for controlling Windows (see section 1.3 for details).

3 Mouse The mouse is the most common method of controlling Windows and software applications. Moving the mouse with either hand controls an on-screen pointer used for selecting items (see section 1.2 for details).

Common peripherals

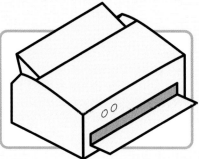

Printers Printers come in many shapes and sizes. The main distinction is between ink-based and laser types. A further difference is that they can be colour or monochrome.

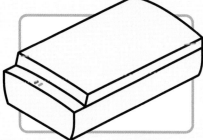

Scanners These devices make digital copies of paper-based images or text, which are transferred to the PC.

Control devices The most common device for controlling PC software is the mouse. For action games, however, a joystick (pictured here) is almost essential, while for graphics artists often use a tablet, which is a bit like an electronic sketch pad.

What's the difference between CD-ROM, DVD and CD-RW drives?

CD-ROM drives can play music, run software or browse stored data. DVD (digital versatile disk) drives play DVD disks, which have a much larger capacity and typically are used for movies and videos. DVDs are increasingly used to supply much bigger programs. CD writers (CD-R and CD-RW) are drives that write to blank CDs. CD-R disks can be written to only once, while CD-RW disks can be written to many times. Recordable DVD drives are appearing on the market.

4 Floppy drive This is where you insert 3¹/₂-inch disks (which are not floppy). They are used mainly for moving information from one computer to another.

5 CD-ROM drive On new PCs this will usually play DVDs. Some suppliers provide a CD-R/CD-RW drive.

6 The internal hard disk This stores the Windows operating system, the software and files. It is hidden inside your PC.

7 Power switch The switch that turns the machine off and on.

8 Reset button When your PC stops responding, this forces it to restart.

9 Hard-disk light This light flickers when the hard disk is active.

10 Speakers Computer speakers are similar to speakers used in hi-fi equipment, but they usually have a volume control dial built into the chassis.

11 Control devices See section on Common peripherals above.

THE MOUSE

Types of mice

Many manufacturers produce a variety of mice. Ergonomic varieties can help reduce repetitive strain injury (RSI). Mice are available for both left- and right-handed users. Wireless mice can help to reduce cable clutter on the desk.

The mouse is the most common way of accessing Windows. Moving the mouse with your hand makes a small pointer move on your screen. A mouse has either two or three buttons, each of which, when pressed, performs a different action on the item you have selected. The mouse can be used to manipulate files, control software and access the features of Windows.

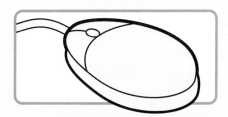

A typical mouse

Left button The left mouse button is used mainly for selecting an item. Note that a mouse for a left-handed person has the functions reversed.

Right button The right mouse button when clicked on an item normally brings up more information about the item and often additional menus for controlling the features of the selected item.

Centre button or wheel Some mice also have a centre button or wheel in between the left and right mouse buttons. This third controller often provides a short cut for scrolling a window up or down, while also acting as a trigger button in computer games.

Mouse cursor shapes and what they mean
The mouse regulates a cursor which changes shape depending on what your computer is doing or what item the mouse is resting on.

 This pointer is the most common type of mouse cursor and is used to select menus, files and options.

 You see this when you click on the Help menu, select **'What's this?'** and choose an item.

 The cursor looks like this if you try to select features in Windows that are not available.

 This hourglass symbol appears when Windows is busy doing something. You have to wait for the system to finish its task before doing anything else.

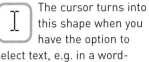 The cursor turns into this shape when you have the option to select text, e.g. in a word-processing package.

 The cursor changes into one of these shapes when you move it to the edge of a window to change the size of folders or application windows.

 The cursor looks like this when you hold down the left mouse button on the edge of a folder so you can move it round the desktop.

 This signifies a link to a web page or another file.

Examples of mouse usage

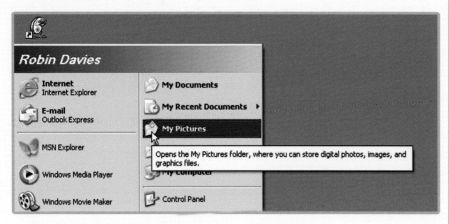

Using the left click Clicking the left mouse button once generally selects a file, application or menu option.

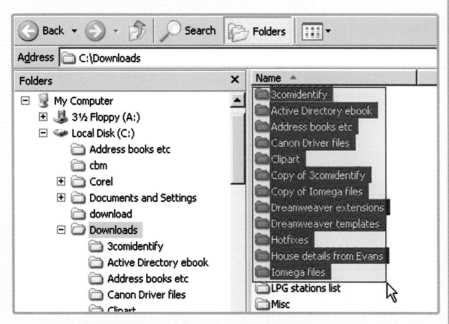

Double-clicking means clicking on an item twice in quick succession. This action on an icon opens the folder, runs the application or selects the menu option.

Holding down the left mouse button and moving the mouse allows you to select/highlight multiple files or menus that are adjacent to one another. If you want to select files or folders that are not next to one another, hold down the Ctrl key when clicking the left mouse button. You can then click the right mouse button and choose an option such as copy, cut or paste and apply that to the whole group you have selected.

Warning!

To prevent your mouse becoming dirty use a plastic mouse mat, which you should clean about once a month. Refer to the manufacturer's instructions on how to clean the ball and rollers of the mouse itself.

THE KEYBOARD

Keyboard essentials

A modern UK PC keyboard has at least 102 keys. Some PCs have extra keys for special functions such as sending emails or playing music. Some keys, as you can see in the diagram, are duplicated.

The keyboard has two main uses — to type characters into software programs such as word processors or spreadsheets, and to access features of the software or change their settings. A computer keyboard is similar to a typewriter, but it has additional features. This section describes the functions of some of the most commonly used keys. Some keys, such as Alt, Tab, Insert, Page Up and Page Down, do different things in different applications.

1 Escape key (Esc) The Escape key has several different uses. In many applications Esc will end a program or cancel a task.

2 QWERTY keys The most popular type of keyboard starts with the letters Q, W, E, R, T and Y on the fourth row from the bottom. This is based on the arrangement of letters on a typewriter.

3 Punctuation marks and operators This group of keys includes punctuation marks and special symbols like @ and ~. The top ones are obtained by pressing the key while holding down the Shift key.

4 Return/Enter The Enter and Return keys are used to select an option from a menu or to move the cursor to a new line. They are generally interchangeable.

Warning!

Pressing keys on the keyboard while your PC is starting up can prevent the PC from starting up correctly.

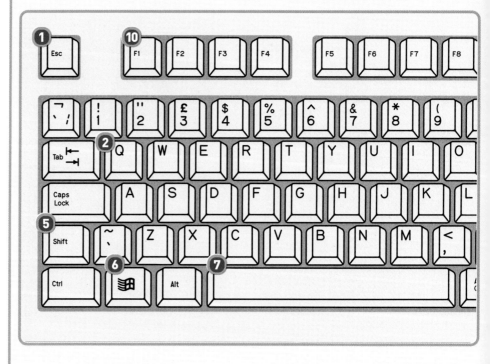

5 **Caps Lock/Shift key** The Shift key when held down while pressing another key produces an alternative character for the second key (e.g. pressing the 'Q' key normally produces 'q', but with the Shift key it produces 'Q' in upper case). The Caps Lock key when depressed allows you to type a number of characters in upper case.

6 **Start/Windows key** When pressed, this key will bring up the main Windows Start menu.

7 **Space bar** When pressed, this bar produces a blank character in word-processing, spreadsheet and database applications.

8 **Control key (Ctrl)** This is often used in conjunction with another key to access a shortcut (e.g. holding down Ctrl while pressing 'B' creates bold text in most word-processing software).

9 **Numeric keypad** The numeric keypad allows quick entry of numbers. This is especially useful for data entry on to spreadsheets.

10 **Function keys F1 to F12** Function keys often act as shortcuts to activate different parts of a program (e.g. F1 normally brings up on-screen help).

A keyboard to suit you

Keyboards come in various guises. Some are specially designed as ergonomic keyboards that can help reduce strain on the wrists and hands of people who type for long periods. Wireless keyboards are becoming popular. Not only do they reduce cable clutter on your desk, but you can sit some metres away from your desk, even in your armchair!

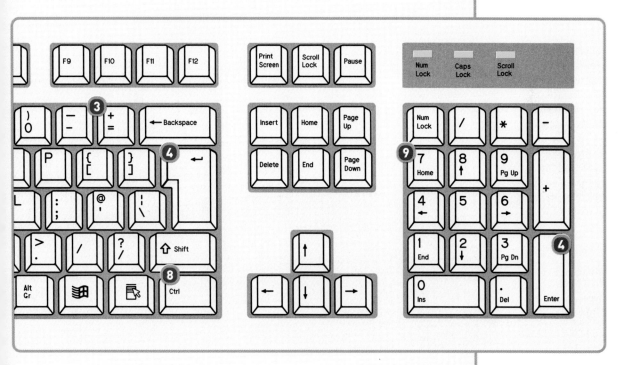

THE WINDOWS XP OPERATING SYSTEM

In the beginning . . .

The original Windows version 1.0 was sold in 1985. Version 3.0 was released in 1990 and the first really popular version, 3.1, sold a then-unheard-of 1 million copies within two months when it came out in 1992. Windows 95 managed the same feat within four days.

Microsoft Windows is the most common operating system on home PCs. Windows XP (released in October 2001) provides an easy-to-learn and intuitive interface for working with software and hardware. XP is much more colourful than earlier editions of Windows, and you can easily customise it to your individual tastes and needs. If you prefer the look of older versions (98 or ME) you can choose the Classic view inside most windows. More important than the way Windows XP looks, it is much more stable and robust than Windows 95, 98 and ME. This is because it is built on the code of Windows 2000, which was designed for business use and was therefore stronger.

Unlike Windows 95, 98 or ME, Windows XP requires you to tell it who you are by logging on to your account. This is great for a family PC, because it means that each member of the family can have his or her own XP account and arrange how XP works to suit his or her own tastes. Having separate accounts for everybody who uses a PC means that each user's settings and work can be protected against accidental (or deliberate!) alteration by somebody else.

This section shows the first screen you see after logging on to XP. This is called the desktop.

What are icons?

An icon is a picture that represents a link to software or documents. Double-clicking on an icon normally launches the program or opens up the document.

In all versions of Windows from 95 onwards, the desktop displays two things: first, the icons, which are shortcuts to programs you may wish to use, and second, the Start button, which is found at the bottom of the screen in the taskbar and on the left-hand side of the screen. You will notice that this button can be found on each side of the keyboard. Pressing this button displays the Start menu. In Windows XP a window opens on the desktop.

Free Windows XP tour

When you first get your PC, if you click the 'Start' button in XP, you can take a tour of XP by clicking on 'Tour Windows XP'.

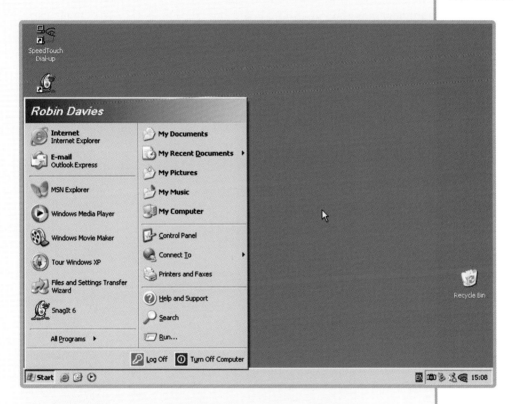

Why is it called a desktop?

The main Windows interface is designed to be an electronic version of your desk and you can manage it and organise it in a personal way. It can be clean and tidy or cluttered and messy!

Taskbar

The Windows XP taskbar, which runs all along the bottom of your screen, contains three elements. On the extreme left is the Start button. To the right of it are boxes showing the programs currently running. Over on the right is the notification area, which shows system applications that

are running in the background. Right-clicking or double left-clicking an icon generally launches a configuration program which allows you to change settings.

Double left-clicking on the time function brings up a small calendar with options for setting time, date and geographical time zone.

THE WINDOWS DESKTOP (I)

Differences between Windows XP and Windows 98 and ME

While the visual differences between Windows 98 and Windows ME are relatively minor, XP has a radically new 'look and feel'. The changes within XP are not cosmetic, but a fundamental change delivering the two vital elements of reliability and user-friendliness. However, many of the old favourites are still there and, if you are upgrading from an earlier version, it is very easy to apply a Windows 'classic' interface. See section 2.10 for more on the differences.

This section (and the following one) describes in detail the features of the Windows XP desktop. If you are used to an earlier version of Windows, you will notice considerable differences. Microsoft has gone to great lengths to make XP both user-friendly and the desktop easy to customise. The Start button is a logical entry point and the Start window that pops up in XP allows easy access to the major tasks you are likely to want to complete.

How to organise folders

When you create a file, e.g. a letter to your bank, using word-processing software, you could name it 'bankletter01'. You could then choose to place it in a folder called 'letters', which has all your other letters in it. You could then create another folder

called 'personal' and put the 'letters' folder in it. In this example, the 'letters' folder is a sub-folder of the 'personal' folder.

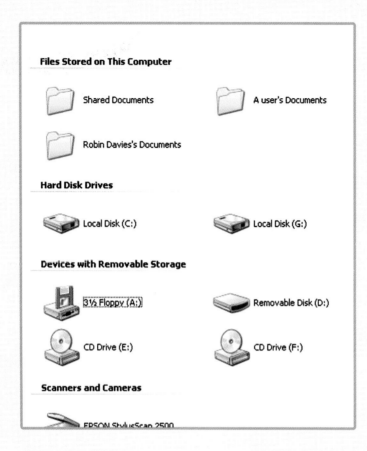

Help at hand

All versions of Windows offer built-in help. For Windows itself you can access help in two ways. Either just press the F1 key or click on 'Start' and choose 'Help'. In Windows XP it is called 'Help and Support'. If you need help in a Windows program, the simplest thing to do is press the F1 button for help. You can also normally select the Help menu in most Windows programs.

Different kinds of icons

A variety of icons is shown above. Every item in Windows has an icon that normally represents what the item contains. You can see in the next section that in Windows XP they are self-explanatory.

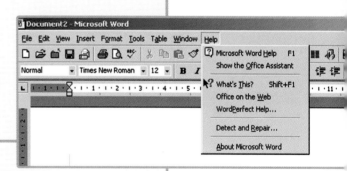

THE WINDOWS DESKTOP (II)

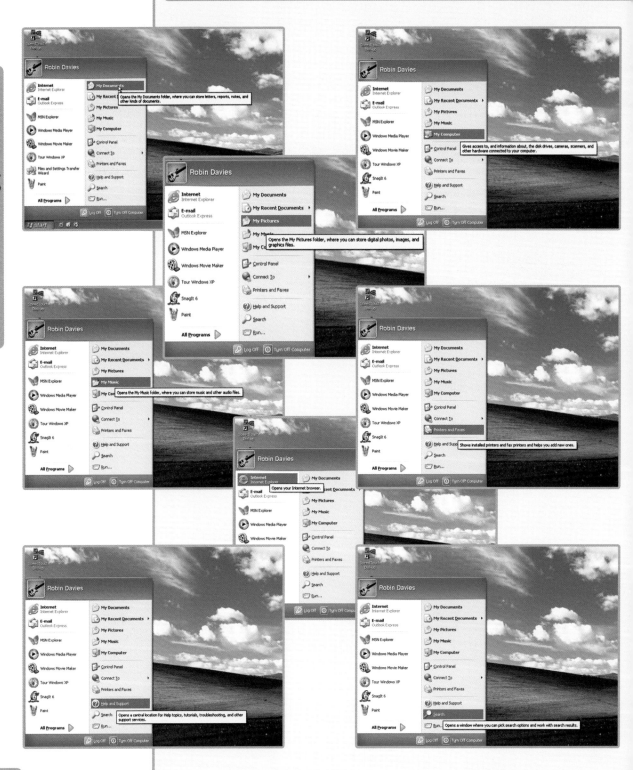

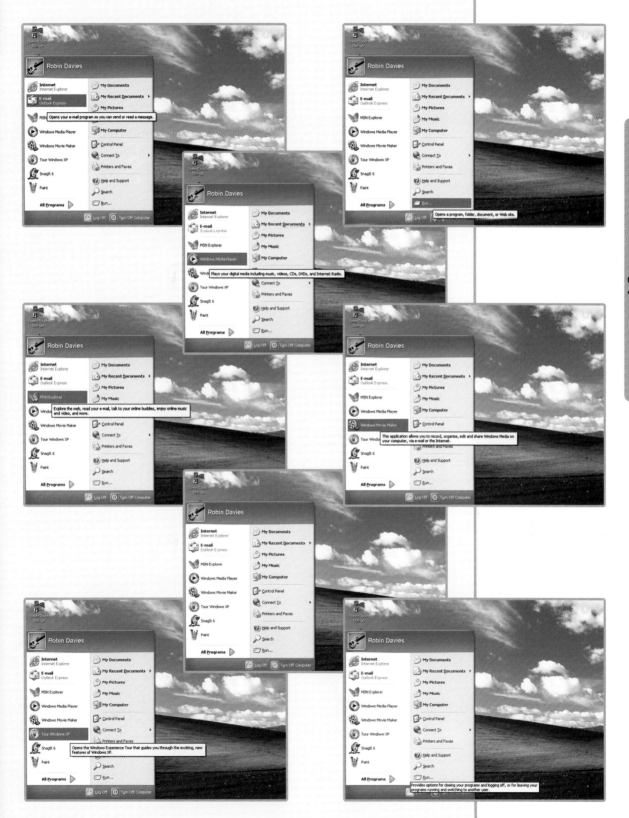

BUILT-IN APPLICATIONS

Buying a PC is really only the beginning. In order to do anything with the PC, you need software (also called programs, applications or packages). This section looks at the applications that are supplied with Windows itself. Although this book concentrates on Windows XP, all recent versions of Windows have built-in applications and, in many cases, they have the same names.

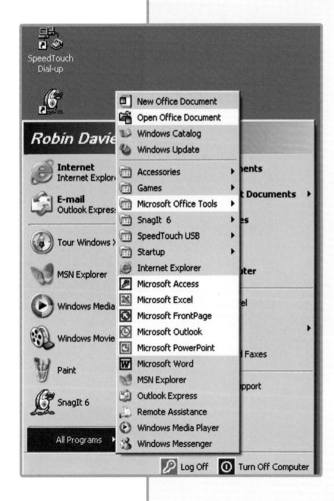

In XP they can be found by clicking on '**Start**' and then on '**All Programs**'.

From the menu that pops up, choose '**Accessories**'.

In the list of programs that now appears, you will notice two programs which work with words (Notepad and WordPad), a drawing program called Paint and other programs which work with sounds, music and video.

WordPad is an adequate word-processing program which has been supplied with Windows since before Windows 95. In Windows XP it is more integrated with the Internet than earlier versions and you can email files created in WordPad direct from the File menu.

WordPad – a basic word processor

Control menu These three icons from left to right are used to minimise the window (which reduces the document to an icon on the taskbar at the bottom of the screen), maximise the window (so it takes up the full dimension of the screen) and close the application respectively. Most Windows applications have these control icons present.

Toolbars
Most software applications have a number of icons which allow you to access different functions quickly. In this word processor, you can change the font from Times New Roman by clicking once on the down-arrow icon to the right of the font description and choosing one of the options that comes up.

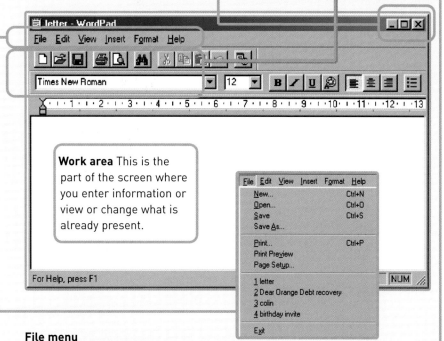

Work area This is the part of the screen where you enter information or view or change what is already present.

Suite spot

Many software suppliers group applications together in suites. The most common and popular suite is Microsoft Office; others include Lotus SmartSuite and Star Office. Microsoft also has a less weighty product called Works, which is often pre-installed on new PCs. It is more than adequate for most uses. Menus, icons and styles are often the same within a suite and data is usually designed to be transferable from one application in a suite to another.

File menu

Most Windows software applications have a menu system (or a series of options) for accessing features of the program. Normally this starts with the File menu.

The File menu contains options for you to create a new file, open an existing one or save one that is currently in use.

Most applications allow you to send contents to a printer. Moreover, by using the **'Print Preview'** option you can see what the document will look like when it is printed.

The names of the last few documents that you worked on are shown here; as a shortcut you could click on one to open it up.

The File menu usually has an option to exit the software.

INSTALLING AND REMOVING APPLICATIONS

Free software

Some software suppliers offer earlier versions of their programs over the Internet or on magazine CDs. These old, but fully working, versions are not supported by the suppliers but can offer big savings over buying a suite.

Magazine CDs

Most computer magazines come with CDs on the cover. These hold masses of software which you can try at no cost (other than that of buying the magazine). Some are really free, many are 'shareware' and others are time- or feature-limited demos.

Shareware

This way of acquiring software is not, as is commonly thought, free. The philosophy of shareware is 'try, then buy'. Much of this software is of the highest quality and very useful. It is usually really cheap (normally priced in dollars) and you can pay for it online with a credit card.

Tens of thousands of software applications that work with Windows are available. Some will come with your PC, but adding more is easy and limited only by the depth of your wallet and the space on your hard disk! These days software is normally supplied on one or more CDs but, increasingly, people download software directly to their PC from the Internet. Payment is made by credit card using secure servers.

Each program usually comes with its own instructions for installation (normally by inserting a CD into the drive and following the on-screen instructions), but you have to be able to work out if your machine is capable of running the new software correctly. Generally a software supplier will list the minimum configuration required to run its package. As software programs seem to grow in size, you may need to clear some disk space in order to make way for new software. On new PCs you are likely to have enough space on your hard disk, but remember, hard disks do not magically get bigger!

Installing software

The most common method for installing software is using a CD-ROM. Placing a disk containing software into the CD-ROM drive normally automatically installs the software. If the software fails to start, click on '**Start**', then '**My Computer**' and then on the CD-ROM to open up the main directory of the disk. This directory should contain a file called either '**Setup**' or '**Install**'; selecting one of these files normally loads the software on to your PC. See section 7.5 on downloading software from the Internet.

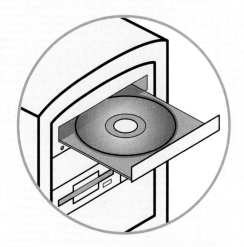

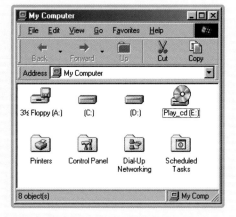

Removing software

To install or remove a program you need to go to the Windows Control Panel. To do this in Windows XP click on **'Start'**, then **'Control Panel'**. In Windows 98 click on **'Start'**, **'Settings'** and then **'Control Panel'**. The Control Panel contains numerous icons, each representing a different application. Find the **'Add/Remove Programs'** icon and double-click on it.

The **'Add/Remove Programs'** window has three main areas.

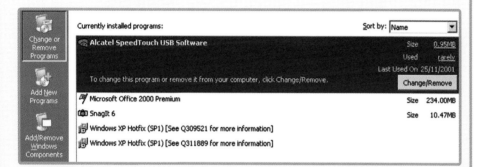

'Change or Remove Programs'
This is where you select programs for removal.

'Add New Programs' This is rarely used as almost all programs today come with their own installation routines on the CD. These start after you place the CD in the CD-ROM drive and close the tray.

'Add/Remove Windows Components'
This allows you to make changes to Windows.

Windows 98

For the slightly different way that Windows 98 works, see section 1.11.

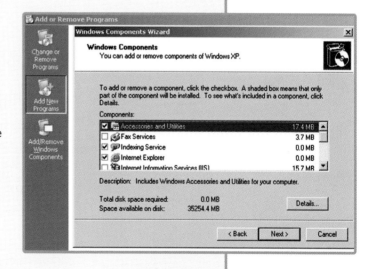

ADDING HARDWARE TO YOUR PC

The USB advantage

Universal serial bus (USB) is the easiest and most popular way to connect peripherals to a PC. Its main advantages over the older serial and parallel ports are speed and connectivity. USB is about 100 times faster than a serial port and you can connect over 20 devices simultaneously. Most PCs come with two USB ports, but more can be added easily. Note that the cheapest printers and scanners may not have a USB port, so always check before buying one.

Warning!

As a safety precaution, you should never plug in or remove peripherals while the system is switched on. The exception to this rule is USB, which is specifically designed for plugging in while the PC is still on (often referred to as 'hot swapping').

Various items of hardware, such as printers and scanners, can be attached to your computer to provide extra facilities. Each item, known as a peripheral or add-on, connects to your PC via a cable plugged into a socket at the rear of your machine. A peripheral requires software to allow Windows to control it. It may also have minimum requirements in terms of computer memory or processor speed, so before buying a new peripheral you need to check whether your PC can support it (that it is 'compatible' with the peripheral). Some peripherals are described in section 1.1; this section looks at other common ones and shows the sockets used to connect them. How to check on whether your PC is compatible with a peripheral is covered in the next section.

Common PC peripherals

Personal organisers Modern personal organisers or personal digital assistants (PDAs) work in harmony with PCs. If you connect your PDA to your PC (using the connection recommended for that make), calendars and documents on both the machines can be synchronised, such that any changes on one

will be automatically made on the other.
Digital camera The boom in digital photography has been fuelled by the huge potential cost savings over traditional chemical prints. Digital cameras hold pictures electronically and can transfer large amounts of data to the PC for editing. They often use the USB port for improved speed.

Projector A projector equipped with a compatible VGA (see opposite) port can be connected to your PC. Although it is quite expensive, it is useful for training purposes in offices, and also for certain games. A projector will plug directly into the

display adapter of the PC graphics card.
Backup tape/disk/CD-writers Hard disks can fail, rendering files unreadable. Backup drives are commonly used to store copies of important files such as invoices, letters and accounts. With the right software you can write a complete image of your hard disk to a CD-writer. See section 2.3 for more on backups.

Interfaces for connecting PC peripherals

VGA/Display The VGA connector has 15 pins and is where the monitor is connected. Some graphics cards have two of these sockets, allowing dual monitors. This is possible only with Windows 98 or later versions of Windows.

Parallel/LPT The parallel interface, a 25-pin connector, is generally used to connect the printer, but can also be used for scanners, tape backup units and a host of other peripherals.

Serial/COM The serial port is the oldest and most versatile connector for the PC. Often referred to as the communications port, it can also provide a low-speed connection between computers via either cables or modems. It can have 9 (as shown) or 25 holes.

PS/2/Mouse/Keyboard The PS/2 socket is used mostly for keyboards and mice. Unfortunately, the sockets for both devices are identical and getting them mixed up is one of the most common technical support problems when users first set up new machines.

USB Universal serial bus (USB) is a high-speed version of the serial port, and is standard on all new PCs. It is great for printers, scanners, digital cameras and video devices.

MIC input/Line input/Line output Essentially these ports are similar to headphone sockets and provide connections for audio devices such as microphones, speakers and amplifiers. PC manufacturers either colour-code or label each port to avoid confusion between the microphone and speaker sockets.

Internal and external peripherals

With some computer peripherals you have a choice of whether to have an internal version (which resides within the chassis of the PC) or an external one. Often internal devices have a speed advantage or a cost-saving.

Common examples of internal devices include tape backup units or CD-writers. When deciding on whether to buy an internal or external device, bear in mind that:

- internal devices can be more complicated to fit and may also need free spaces and appropriate mounting kits within the PC's chassis

- external devices can be shared between PCs or laptops but they are often significantly more expensive and mostly slower. You would also need to install the software for each device on every PC the device uses.

CHECKING YOUR PC's SPECIFICATIONS

When a peripheral, such as a printer, scanner or digital camera, is attached to your PC it makes demands on the machine in terms of memory, so you need to be sure that your PC has sufficient memory to support it. Also, how well a peripheral functions may depend on the speed of your computer. Most PCs are compatible with printers; new machines normally can support additional peripherals such as scanners and speakers. However, if you wish to attach a new peripheral to your machine you must check that your machine has the resources to support it.

For example, with Windows XP, you need 64Mb RAM for every active user account. So if every member of a family of four has a separate account, the PC will need a minimum of 256Mb RAM. It would be easiest to have that extra RAM added when you are buying a new PC, although you could add it to an existing machine (see section 6.1).

Specification sheet

When you buy a new PC, you will be provided with a specification sheet that lists the speed and type of the processor (e.g. 1.2GHz Athlon), the amount of memory (RAM) measured in megabytes (e.g. 128Mb) and the capacity of the hard-disk drive measured in gigabytes (e.g. 20Gb, which is 20,000Mb). The list will include the type of graphics card and the extra devices, such as modems and DVD drives, that come with your PC.

Double-clicking on the **'My Computer'** icon and then selecting **'View System Information'** displays the **'System Properties'** window. This is probably the most important configuration screen and contains information about all your hardware and other Windows settings.

The **'Hardware'** tab displays the **'Add Hardware Wizard'** (which walks you through installing new hardware), the **'Device Manager'** and **'Hardware Profiles'**.

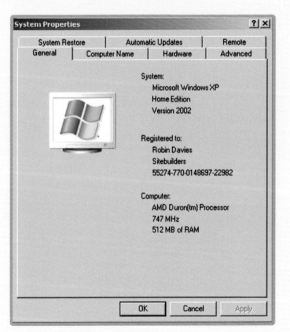

Device Manager

The **'Device Manager'** button lists all the devices that Windows believes are installed on the system and also whether each device appears to be working.

Each device belongs to a group, e.g. disk drives or display adapters; a group can contain more than one device. Clicking on the + symbol on the left of a group lists all the devices within that group.

Right-clicking on a device and selecting **'Properties'** displays

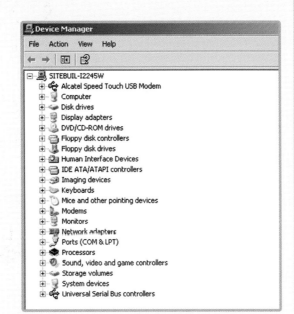

more detailed information and allows you to change the

device's configuration. This is covered in more depth in section 5.7.

Identifying the chip

In Windows 98 and ME you may find when you click on the **'General'** tab of the 'System Properties' screen in the Control Panel that your chip is wrongly identified – e.g. your CPU may actually be made by AMD but may be shown as an Intel processor. This is because the processors are so similar that some versions of Windows cannot distinguish between them. This is not a problem in either Windows 2000 or Windows XP.

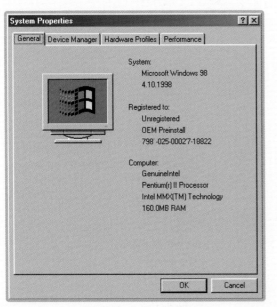

Earlier versions of Windows

Earlier versions of Windows (95, 98, ME and 2000) work in very similar ways, although Windows 2000 is a little different from its predecessors (and more like Windows XP). This is what the Windows 98 **'System Properties'** looks like.

Warning!

Unless you are constantly experiencing problems with your hard disk, you are advised not to change settings within the FileSystem/ Troubleshooting menu as this can cause Windows to start up incorrectly.

THE DESKTOP IN WINDOWS 98

What differences?

Because they use the same code base, Windows 95, 98 and ME have great similarities. In fact, Windows ME has been described as 'Windows 98 Third Edition'. It features a System Restore feature, silent installation of USB keyboards, mice and hubs, a Movie Maker application for recording, editing, publishing and organising audio and video content, the removal of real mode DOS, and a number of other small improvements. Apart from looking like Windows 2000, it is really 98 in disguise.

The desktop in Windows 95 and both editions of Windows 98 is essentially the same. Double-clicking on any icon starts that program or task. The standard installation of Windows 98 will normally show **'My Computer'** and **'My Documents'**. As in all versions of Windows, the Start menu is a useful way to access all programs, files and documents.

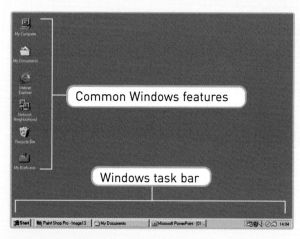

Common Windows features

Windows task bar

The Windows Start menu

Programs lists the software applications installed on the system. Older DOS programs may not always be listed here.

Favorites lists folders created by the 'Add to favorite' option.

Documents displays the most recently used files. Clicking on a file listed here launches the software that the file was created with.

Basic Windows icons

My Computer Clicking twice on this image (called an icon) allows you to explore your computer's hard and other disks. It lists the files and folders on your PC.

My Documents Many Windows applications store files such as letters created using word-processing software in this convenient folder. Clicking twice on this icon shows files stored here.

Internet Explorer Windows 98 comes with a built-in Internet browser. Clicking twice on this icon starts the Internet-browsing software and attempts to make a connection to the Internet.

Network Neighborhood Clicking on this icon lists the computers that are connected to your machine, either over the Internet or via a local area network. For most home users, this feature is not relevant.

Recycle Bin This is a special area of the computer that stores files that have been deleted. Clicking on it twice displays both the files that have been deleted and the option to restore them back into the system.

My Briefcase The briefcase is a way of transferring files from your PC to another computer via a removable disk.

Two versions of Windows 98

Microsoft released a second edition of Windows 98 called, unsurprisingly, Windows 98 SE. It is really Windows 98 first edition with bug fixes and some new functionality (Internet-connection sharing and Internet Explorer 5) packaged as a new Windows release. Certainly Internet Explorer 5 is much better than IE4, and homes with more than one PC could find the Internet-connection sharing facility useful.

Settings helps you customise your PC.

Find is a useful tool for finding files on any drive attached to the computer. See section 2.7 for details.

Help can also be accessed by pressing F1.

Run is most commonly used for running older DOS programs and applications not listed on the Start menu.

Log Off will appear on this menu if you have set up user profiles. If your computer is used by more than one person, user profiles allows each person's settings to be retained.

Shut Down allows Windows to be safely turned off. Modern PCs normally switch themselves off at the end of the shut-down process.

FREQUENTLY ASKED QUESTIONS

Most PC manufacturers provide instructions for setting up a PC for the first time. However, these can sometimes be confusing or not comprehensive enough. This section looks at the problems most commonly experienced by first-time computer users.

PRINTER PROBLEMS

The printer has power and paper but is still not printing. Why is this?
• Make sure the printer has an ink or toner cartridge installed. Check the manual for instructions on how to install consumables. Some printers have clear, picture-driven instructions under the lid of the printer. When you installed the printer you may well have installed software which can clean the inkjet nozzles if the print quality is poor.
• Make sure the printer cable is firmly attached at both ends. Turn your PC off by clicking on **'Start'** at the bottom left-hand corner, then select **'Shut Down'**. After your PC has shut down, turn the power back on and test the printer again. Do not use the **'Restart'** option, because only a full shutdown will send a reset command to the printer.
• Check that the printer driver is installed and that the printer is selected.

The printer is loaded with paper, so why, when I try to print, does the computer tell me that it is 'out of paper'?
• Try using fewer sheets of paper in the feeder.
• Many printers have two separate paper feeds, one for single sheets (often used for letterheads) and a main feeder for multiple sheets of paper. Try putting paper in both of these feeds and testing the printer again.

The printer will not feed the paper through and an error light is flashing.
• Check carefully for foreign bodies in the paper path – especially where the paper enters the printer. If you had a paper jam and tore the paper when removing a stuck sheet, check that no tiny pieces were left behind.

MOUSE PROBLEMS

Moving the mouse does not move the pointer on the screen. Why is this?
• The mouse and keyboard sockets often look very similar. Try swapping over the mouse and keyboard cables and restarting the PC.
• Some mice come with a protective shield. Turn the mouse upside-down and make sure that the mouse ball can spin freely. If not, open the bottom of the mouse to inspect it, and remove any fluff or dirt that is obstructing the ball.
• Some types of mouse use the serial ports (see section 1.9). Systems normally have two of these ports. Try the mouse in each port, restarting the PC each time.

SOUND PROBLEMS

The speakers are connected to the base unit, so why is no sound coming from my PC?
• Some computer speakers, unlike hi-fi speakers, have a separate on/off switch and volume controls. Make sure that these are correctly set.
• Some speakers need a separate power supply or even batteries: check that you have powered your speakers correctly.
• The PC has up to three audio sockets: one for speakers, one for a microphone and an additional socket for line-out. Test the speakers in each socket as these are often unlabelled. It is very easy to plug speakers into the wrong socket accidentally.
• Test your speakers with a Walkman to make sure they haven't blown.
• Make sure that the Windows volume control is set correctly and that the mute box is not checked. You can activate this control by clicking on the small speaker icon in the bottom right-hand corner of your desktop. Also check the full mixer controls.

SCREEN/MONITOR PROBLEMS

There is power going to both my PC and the computer monitor, but nothing appears. Why?
• Try adjusting the brightness and contrast controls on the front of your monitor.
• Make sure that the cable between your PC system unit and the monitor is firmly attached, then restart your PC.

Part of the Windows desktop is running off the edge of the monitor. Why?
• The controls at the front of your monitor allow you to alter the position of the Windows screen in relation to your monitor's centre. Refer to the manual which accompanied your monitor, under **'resize/controls'**.

WINDOWS PROBLEMS

My monitor, keyboard and mouse are all connected but Windows still won't start. Why?
• Make sure that there is no floppy disk in the floppy drive when starting the PC.
• Windows may fail to start if the keyboard or mouse are in the wrong port (the mouse and keyboard sockets are often identical). Try swapping them around and then restarting your PC.
• Make sure that none of the keys is jammed in the **'down'** position when you turn on the PC.

GENERAL TIPS

• Always keep all the manuals and software with the PC.
• Most companies which sell PC systems offer free technical support over the phone. Turn to your supplier first of all if you have problems in setting up your PC.
• If your PC appears to be totally dead, test the power sockets you are using for your PC with a lamp or alarm clock.

The modern desktop PC is surprisingly self-reliant. The operating system makes regular checks on hardware and software to make sure they are working, while smart applications send information on their status whenever they are used. If a problem does occur, Windows will try to fix it, or prompt the user towards remedial action. Unfortunately, things still do go wrong. Just as cars need regular servicing to keep them running efficiently, computer systems also appreciate preventive care. The housekeeping chores should take only a few minutes each week, but if you do them you will not only become more comfortable with your computer's functions, you will also speed up your system's performance. This chapter also explains the basics of how a computer system works.

HOUSEKEEPING AND QUICK FIXES

2.1 **Inside the computer**
PC technology fundamentals

2.2 **Looking after your hard disk**
The hard disk needs regular servicing:
this section explains how

2.3 **Creating backups**
It is essential to make copies of essential files, in case
your computer fails. This section shows you how

2.4 **Viruses and how to avoid them**
An explanation of computer viruses and how to
protect your PC from them

2.5 **Windows Explorer**
Finding your way round the contents of your
PC's hard disk

2.6 **Working with files (I)**
A computer can have hundreds of thousands of files.
This section helps you to work with files

2.7 **Working with files (II)**
Further advice on file management

2.8 **Moving information between applications**
Cutting, copying, pasting and linking information
between applications

2.9 **Tips and tricks**
Some basic aids to make using Windows easier

2.10 **Differences between XP and older versions of Windows**
Some of the differences between versions of Windows

INSIDE THE COMPUTER

Giving your system a boost

Although computer manufacturers constantly promote the CPU's speed as an indication of the performance of a computer system, RAM memory and graphics chipsets play an equally important part.

You can often increase the performance of a sluggish machine by simply adding more memory as opposed to buying a new system.

Warning!

Most PC manufacturers accept that users will want to upgrade their PCs at some point. However, some vendors withdraw technical support or warranties on systems they deem have been 'tampered' with. Always read accompanying material before opening a PC case.

Every activity performed by a computer can be broken down into three steps: the computer system receives information (input), it performs a task normally using software (process), and then produces a result (output). In the case of writing a letter, the input is your words keyed into the word-processing document; the process is the word processor arranging your text and running a spellcheck; and the output is your finished document or letter emerging from your printer. It is important to understand how different parts of a PC work together to perform a task, especially if you want to customise, upgrade or repair your machine.

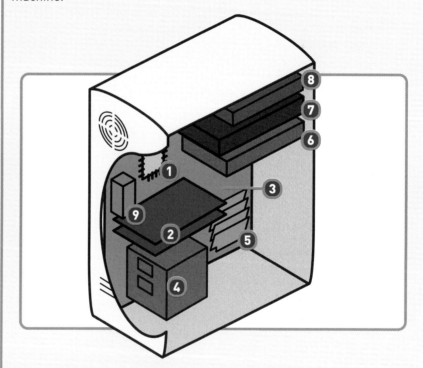

1 Central processing unit (CPU) or processor This chip is the heart of the computer, providing processing power for software applications. The CPU's manufacturer, compatibility type and speed rating (in MegaHertz) are printed on it.

2 AGP/PCI/ISA expansion slots
Most of a PC's flexibility is provided

by these slots. New PCs generally have at least four slots free for a variety of upgrade cards. Common upgrades include graphics, modems, network cards and soundcards.

3 Motherboard
The components of this logic board include the CPU and other chips, memory and expansion slots, and a

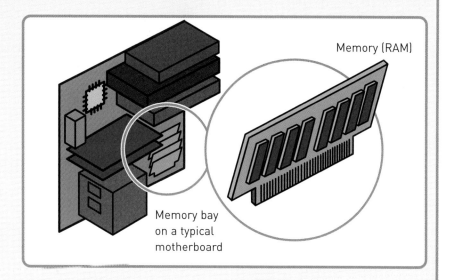

Memory (RAM)

Memory bay
on a typical
motherboard

battery. Newer motherboards can support faster CPUs and more memory.

4 Power supply unit (PSU)

The PSU is a transformer which converts mains into 5v and 12v used by the motherboard and internal devices such as hard- and floppy-disk drives.

5 Memory

The most common type of PC memory is SDRAM, often called DIMMS. These usually come in sticks of multiples of 32Mb. SDRAM is gradually being replaced by DDR (double date rate SDRAM). The minimum RAM size in a modern PC is 128Mb, and 256Mb is becoming increasingly common. Memory holds information only while the power is on, which is why you must save your documents.

6 3½-inch 'floppy' drive

Although by today's standards the capacity of the 3½-inch disk drive is small at 1.44Mb, a disk is exceptionally useful for moving small documents between machines.

7 CD-ROM drive

Most new PCs now come with the choice of a CD-R drive that can not only read standard CD-ROMs but also write to blank disks. They are slower than a hard disk, but are excellent for cheap storage of important files and documents.

8 Hard-disk drive

The hard-disk drive stores the operating system, the software and data that a PC requires to run applications. The drive uses a platter of magnetic disks and a set of read-and-write heads to move information to and from the computer at up to 30Mb per second. The hard disk is resistant to shocks and dirt, but may wear out after about five years' use.

9 Interfaces

Many of the computer's interfaces, such as connections for the keyboard, printer and mouse, are built into the motherboard as standard.

Turning your PC off

It is a myth that computers need to be turned off when not in use. PC systems are designed to be left on permanently and when idle will automatically cut down on the power they draw. However, it is advisable to switch off the monitor, as it uses a lot of energy. See section 3.8 for details.

LOOKING AFTER YOUR HARD DISK

Your PC's hard disk holds software that drives both your PC (Windows) and programs (such as Microsoft Office) which you use to create documents and files. Even a basic new PC comes with a hard disk capable of storing 20,000Mb (20Gb) and so looking after it is essential. All versions of Windows provide basic tools to manage, maintain and repair files and to ensure that your hard disk is performing optimally.

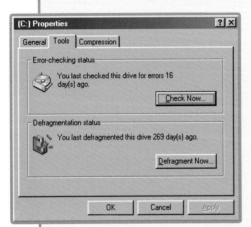

Maintenance options

In the Windows 95, 98 and ME family you reach the maintenance tools by right-clicking on the '**My Computer**' icon and selecting '**Properties**' and then '**Tools**'. This displays the screen on the left.

Warning!

Before starting a scan or defragmentation, make sure you have closed down all applications. This will improve the speed of the scan and the defrag, and prevent the applications from conflicting with the files used by these two programs.

In Windows 2000 and XP things are a little different. Double-click on the '**My Computer**' icon. Use the mouse to point to the selected hard drive (usually C:) and right-click once. Select '**Properties**' and then '**Tools**'.

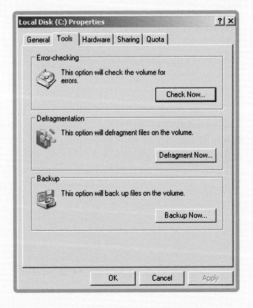

ScanDisk

In all versions of Windows the error-checking program (ScanDisk) looks for corrupted files and repairs them if it can. In earlier versions of Windows you can select automatic repair as well as choosing between a standard check and a more thorough inspection. It is probably worth doing the latter every six months.

Defragmentation

The Defragmentation option reorganises the files on the drive to make them load more quickly. It may not affect the file-loading speed noticeably, but it is useful if you have deleted a lot of files.

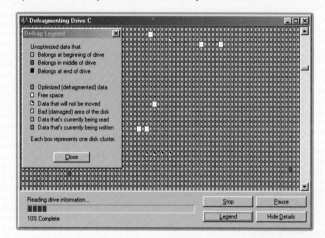

In Windows 2000 and XP the Defragmentation display is completely different, but the effect is the same.

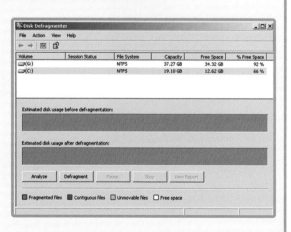

File corruption

Like old vinyl records getting scratched or audiotapes becoming crackly, files can become corrupted through daily usage. On modern computers, file corruption is quite rare. However, viruses or an interruption in power supply could cause corruption.

Prevention is better than cure

Disk scanning and defragmentation should be done regularly – i.e., do not wait until you have a problem. You should run the programs at least once a month, more often if you create and delete files often. See sections 3.6 and 3.7 for details.

CREATING BACKUPS

Types of backup

There are two types of backup you need to make. The first is backups of data files that contain information such as text or pictures; these should be made on a regular basis.

The second kind is a system backup (i.e. of the Windows operating system and applications); you should make this when you first get your system and before you go in for any major hardware.

Installing Backup

Backup is not installed by default in XP Home Edition. You will find the Backup utility on the XP CD. Go to this website for installation instructions:
http://support.microsoft.com/default.aspx?scid=kb;EN-US;q302894

PC systems are much more reliable now than when they first appeared in the early 1980s. However, they still have problems and your system may break down or 'crash' on occasions. The evidence is that Windows XP, like Windows 2000, is a very stable and reliable operating system. If your PC's hardware is of good quality, then the most likely causes of crashes are likely to be poor drivers (software) which run add-ons like new graphics cards, printers and scanners. External problems such as viruses and power failures (never mind your toddler just pulling the power plug out of the socket!) are likely to be the most serious problems you face.

Windows XP can have backup facilities built in. You can back up to floppies, Zip drives, tape drives and another hard disk in your PC. To back up to CD-R you will need to purchase special software and need a CD writer drive. Such software costs about £40 and writes an image of your hard disk to several CDs.

Backing up within Windows XP

To start, click on **'Start'** then **'All Programs'**, **'Accessories'**, **'System Tools'** and **'Backup'**.
The Backup Wizard will appear.

The Wizard will walk you through the process and allow you to back up to a suitable device such as your floppy or a Zip drive.

Types of backup device

CD-ROMs CD writers are CD-ROM drives that can write to a blank disk. There are two types of disks, the CD-R disks (to which you can write only once) and the CD-RW (to which you can write many times). Blank CD-R disks can be bought in bulk for as little as 25p each and will store up to 700Mb of data. Although they are slower than a hard disk, they are reasonably fast. Reliable drives can be purchased for under £80.
Many new PCs come with a CD-R drive, an excellent backup device.

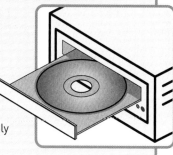

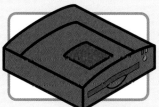

Zip drives Backing up to a Zip drive is a useful alternative. There are currently two different types of internal Zip drives. One stores 100Mb on each Zip disk and the other 250Mb. The 100Mb drive costs about £40 and is gradually dropping out of use. Blank disks cost about £8. The 250Mb-capacity drive costs about £70 for an internal version, with each blank disk costing just under £10. The external versions are twice as expensive and slower.

Tape drives These units can be internal or external. They can be quite fast and store very large amounts of data, are very reliable. However, for the home user they are expensive. The cheapest internal drive costs about £190 and each tape costs about £20. One blank tape for these cheaper drives can store between 4Gb and 8Gb.

Floppy disks These are the easiest and cheapest method of backing up small files, and provide a simple method of transferring information between computers. Each floppy disk holds 1.44Mb. A large Word file with lots of fancy formatting and pictures could easily be too large for one floppy. Basic text-only files are quite small and several will fit on one floppy.

Creating a bootable floppy for Windows XP

In some situations – especially if you appear to have problems with your hard disk – a bootable floppy will allow you to start your PC and check the basics of the machine. Creating one on an XP system is simple. Follow these instructions when you first get your PC.

1. Place a blank disk in the floppy-disk drive.
2. Click '**Start**', and then '**My Computer**'.
3. Right-click the floppy-disk drive, and then click '**Format**' on the shortcut menu.
4. Click '**Create an MS-DOS start-up disk**', and then click '**Start**'.

Alternatively, you can find a utility on this Microsoft website: www.microsoft.com/downloads/release.asp?releaseid=33290

which when downloaded will allow you to create XP set-up disks for a floppy-based installation when you cannot boot from the CD-ROM.

VIRUSES AND HOW TO AVOID THEM

Computer viruses are malicious programs that can potentially damage your PC software and occasionally parts of the hardware too. Although no software can guarantee 100 per cent protection against these programs, you can protect yourself by following the simple steps outlined below.

Virus outbreaks

It is commonly believed that the first computer virus appeared in the 1980s. Two brothers who ran a computer store in an Asian country were fed up with computer piracy. They wrote the first computer virus, a boot-sector virus called Brain. Today, with several new examples appearing each week, there are tens of thousands of viruses.

Computer viruses are a serious and seemingly ever-growing threat. Although some are harmless and just irritating (the WM97/Class-D virus repeatedly displays messages such as 'I think "username" is a big stupid jerk'), many of them are harmful. They can destroy software, wipe out the contents of your hard disk and permanently damage your PC system. The CIH virus attempts to overwrite the Flash BIOS, which can cause irreparable damage to some PCs. Generally, viruses are designed to be self-replicating (i.e., they can multiply and spread rapidly). Viruses infect computers in specific ways and the most common types are macro, boot and parasitic viruses.

Macro viruses

Macros are instructions in a program that make it carry out certain instructions. They are commonly used in word-processors, spreadsheets and slide-presentation programs. Macro viruses are macros that self-replicate. Because people frequently email documents to friends, work colleagues, etc., any document that is infected with a macro virus can spread that virus to recipients very rapidly. Macro viruses are the most common types of viruses.

Boot-sector viruses

When your PC starts up, the first software that is loaded from your PC's hard disk (before Windows) is the boot sector. If there is no boot sector, the PC cannot load any software at all. A boot-sector virus modifies the boot sector on the disk. Most commonly, this type of virus is introduced when a floppy is used to boot a PC. A boot-sector virus cannot infect a PC after Windows has started.

Parasitic viruses

These viruses attach themselves to programs, also known as executables. Parasitic viruses do all sorts of unhelpful things. A well-known example of one in 2001 was Nimda.

Windows has no built-in anti-virus software. This is because, unlike applications, anti-virus software needs to be constantly updated in order to cope with new strains or varieties of viruses. If you buy a new PC the supplier may include some

Ticking bomb . . .

Many viruses come with a 'payload'. This means that they get activated under certain circumstances (e.g. on a particular date or when the hard disk has reached a certain capacity), and then proceed to perform a harmful action such as wiping the disk. Unfortunately, prevention is the only cure.

anti-virus software. However, you must be aware that on the day you take your new PC out of its packaging, this anti-virus software will be out-of-date. Up to 400 new viruses can appear in a single month. Dedicated anti-virus software, easily purchased either over the counter or online, is supplied with regular updates (normally to be downloaded from the Internet). You will find a list of useful websites at the end of the book.

The solution

Virus-protection software is neither 100 per cent effective nor free. The best is very, very good and the costs are low. You can buy all you need for £25 per year or less. Most suppliers provide a year's worth of free updates via their websites – by checking regularly for updates you can keep abreast of developments.

You can protect yourself to a high degree by following these steps:

● Avoid downloading .EXE files from websites you are not familiar with or if the site does not offer secure payment facilities. If you are referred to a website for software from a trusted third party, then look for references on the new site to anti-virus checking. Sites such as www.cnet.com are well known and can be trusted as a gateway to lots of safe downloads.

● Change the boot-up sequence so that rather than booting from drive A: if you leave a floppy in your machine by mistake, you boot by default from drive C: instead. This should stop boot-sector viruses (such as Form, CMOS4, AntiCMOS and Monkey) from infecting your PC. In any case, you should never leave a floppy in your system at shutdown.

● Never open files with a double file extension (e.g., message.txt.vbs).

● Never run, download or forward any executables, documents, spreadsheets, etc. that you were not expecting to receive by mail. Anything that runs on your PC should be virus checked and approved first. This is true even if the email appears to come from a named person you know. Viruses such as Badtrans are good at appearing to be plausible emails.

● Keep your anti-virus software up-to-date. It is worth checking for updates at least weekly and probably daily. Usually it is a simple process once you are connected to the Internet.

● JPG, GIF and MP3 files cannot be infected with a virus, but viruses can be disguised as these file types. Jokes, pictures, graphics, screensavers and movie files should be treated with the same amount of suspicion as other file types.

● Trust nobody! Well, trust no emails. If your best friend's PC is infected, then anything sent to you will also be infected.

● After installation of your anti-virus package and a thorough scan by it of all files on your PC, back up important data. If you have a CD-RW drive, back up an image of your hard drive to CD-ROM.

● Keeping Windows up-to-date can be important as Microsoft regularly issues patches to block problems with viruses attacking its software. Windows XP can be configured to auto-update itself (see section 4.11).

WINDOWS EXPLORER

Quicker than a mouse

To access Windows Explorer quickly, press and hold the 'Start' key on the keyboard and also press the 'E' key. Once you have done this a few times, it is very quick. Try using the left thumb and middle finger.

Today's PCs have the capacity to store masses of files: documents, pictures and sounds created by you and anyone else who uses your machine. As well as all those files, there are all the programs stored on the hard disk. How do you find them? How do you organise where they are stored? Well, during the installation process, program files normally put themselves where they should be. It is the files users create that can be a problem.

Windows Explorer is designed to help in this process. The **'My Computer'** and **'My Documents'** icons are the other tools you need for the job.

Where is Windows Explorer?

In Windows XP Microsoft has rather hidden it away, to encourage you to use My Computer and My Documents. In earlier versions, such as Windows ME and Windows 2000, it is accessed by clicking on **'Start'**, **'Programs'**, **'Accessories'** and **'Windows Explorer'**. The fastest way in is to use the technique in the sidebar (left). This is what you will see in Windows XP.

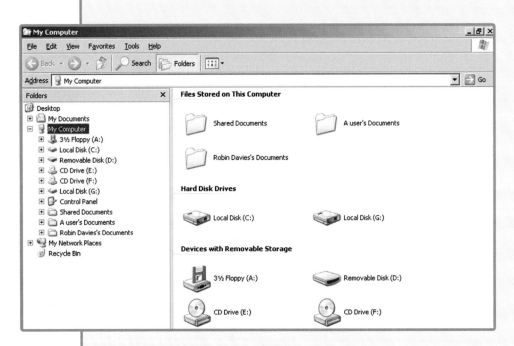

You will notice that the window below is labelled **'My Computer'**, but it is a different view from the one you see if you click on **'Start'** and **'My Computer'**.

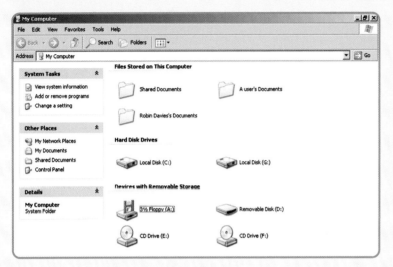

The window displayed when you click on **'Start' + 'E'** shows a little '+' sign next to each drive letter. Click once on the '+' next to drive C.
◀ This is what you will see.

Clicking on the '+' sign expands all drive views and clicking on the '-' sign does the opposite. Try it out. ▶

Is Explorer for me?

How you 'explore' your drives is a matter of personal preference, and with Windows Explorer, My Documents and My Computer there is a range of choices to suit everybody. Experienced computer users often go for keyboard shortcuts as they are often quicker than using a mouse. A lot depends on what you want to do. In the following two sections (Working with files, I and II) you will find some ideas on how to work with files.

WORKING WITH FILES (I)

Other ways to delete files

You can delete files from within the Load-and-save option found on the File menu of many applications. Select a file from within these menus and press the **'delete'** key. Note that deleting files in this way may remove your option to retrieve them via the Recycle Bin.

How to retrieve a deleted file

Provided you have not already emptied the Recycle Bin, you can retrieve a file you have deleted by opening up the bin, right-clicking on the relevant file icon and choosing **'Restore'**. This will result in the file being placed back in the directory you deleted it from.

Files are stored on your PC's hard disk in their thousands. With a new PC, most of these files are going to be program files for the software supplied with the PC. However, once you – and perhaps members of your family – start using the PC, lots of new files will be created and saved. It is important to know what the most common file types are and which programs are likely to have created them.

If you are using a PC in a small business or are working at home, the chances are that you have three sorts of files: documents, financial information and emails. In a home situation you may also have music, graphics and video files. The properties of a Word file are described below.

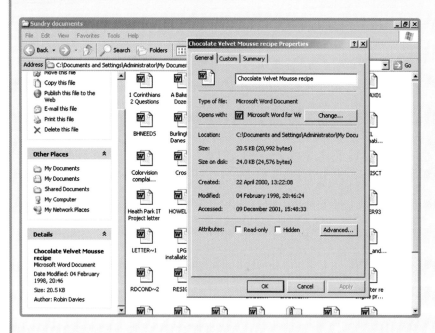

Properties of files

Each file, folder and application normally has an associated properties file, which conveys important information about the item and when it was created. To access an item's properties, right-click on its name and left-click on **'Properties'**. Some programs run configuration programs instead of showing file properties. These configuration programs allow you to change the settings of an application, much like the options on a menu bar. If you do not want to change any option, just click on an empty part of the desktop.

1 This describes the file or folder name and can be up to 256 characters in length.

2 The file type is the most important property. Windows XP shows clearly what program opens this file (Word) but the button allows you to change that if you wish.

3 Here XP shows you where the file is and some information about its size. This section in XP displays file creation and editing information.

4 The Attributes function allows you to alter the properties of a file. Read-only files give additional warnings if you try to delete them, archive files are used in conjunction with backup devices, while hidden files are not shown in directory displays but remain on the hard disk.

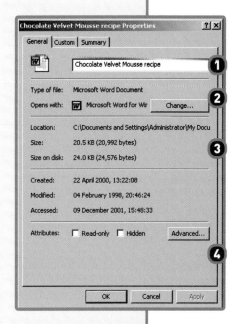

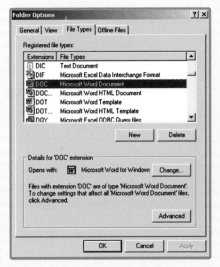

Types of files

Go to **'My Documents'**, and from the menu at the top of the screen, select **'Tools'** and **'Folder Options'**. You will see a tab called **'File Types'**, which will display a long list of file types.

WORKING WITH FILES (II)

Compression

When Windows 95 appeared it contained an option to compress files on a hard disk in order to increase space (called variously 'Compression Agent' or 'Drive Space'). Although this option was retained in 'Start', 'Programs', 'Accessories' and 'System Tools' for the whole Windows 95/98 and ME family, it disappears from the list in Windows 2000 and Windows XP. The simple reason for this is that the increasing size of hard disks and their falling costs makes compressing drives unnecessary.

Working with files is not just a case a knowing where they are or what programs own them, it is also a case of knowing something about the space on your drive. Click on '**Start**' and then '**My Computer**'. Find your hard-disk drive (normally called 'C:') and right-click on the icon. This will display the following window.

Note that despite what is said on the left, an option for disk compression remains, but its use is not advised. You will see in the graphic on the right that most of the hard disk is unused, despite the fact that there are nearly 6,000 files on the hard drive. Knowing how much space you have left can be very important if you, or another user, wish to start saving music, graphic or video files.

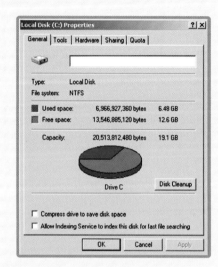

Finding files with the Search facility

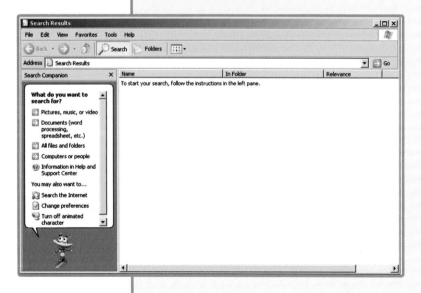

Given that you may have large numbers of files on your computer, using Windows Explorer, My Computer or My Documents to find a specific document may be rather like looking for the proverbial needle. Even XP's My Recent Documents may not help. Instead, try searching. In Windows 95 and 98 click on '**Start**' and '**Find**'. In Windows ME, 2000 and XP, click on '**Start**' and '**Search**'.

XP offers a number of search activities. Start by selecting 'Documents' and entering appropriate criteria.

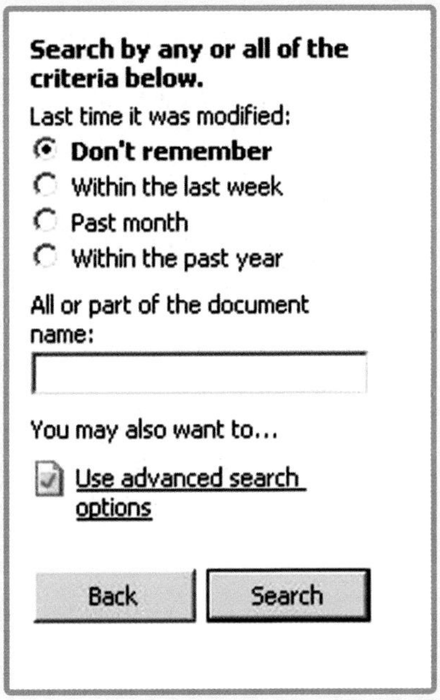

Search by any or all of the criteria below.

Last time it was modified:
- ◉ **Don't remember**
- ○ Within the last week
- ○ Past month
- ○ Within the past year

All or part of the document name:

You may also want to...

☑ Use advanced search options

| Back | Search |

How much free space is left on the hard-disk drive?

To find out how much space you have left on your computer's hard disk, double-click on the '**My Computer**' icon, then right-click on the appropriate drive and select '**Properties**'. This can tell you how much free space is available and also has a useful pie chart — a graphic representation of the amount of space left on the drive.

Using wildcards for more powerful searching

When filling in the name of the file or the file type you are looking for, instead of using whole words you can specify parts of words or groups of files. Below are examples of several types of 'wildcards'.

*.DOC   This option will list all files with the .DOC extension created by Microsoft Word.

WIN.*   This will list all files which have the letters WIN in any part of the name. The final * indicates that all types of file should be listed.

S?N.*   The '?' used in this wildcard means that the character between the 'S' and the 'N' can be anything. So any file names with the words 'sun', 'sin', 'son', etc. will be listed with this search.

MOVING INFORMATION BETWEEN APPLICATIONS

Creating shortcuts

In Windows 98, ME, 2000 and XP you can easily create shortcuts for programs already installed by clicking on **'Start'** and then pointing to the program icon. Hold the left mouse button down and drag the program icon over to the desktop. Let go and a new shortcut icon will appear on the desktop.

A key facility that Windows provides is one called the Clipboard. This allows information to be copied, cut and pasted between programs. The steady move towards integration in the various suites of programs such as Microsoft Office has also made it easier to move information about. At its simplest, this allows a Word document to contain data from a spreadsheet (numbers and charts created from those numbers). Imagine that the Word document is a report on a company's financial position. Naturally, it contains tables and charts created in Excel (the Office spreadsheet). While the document and the spreadsheet are separate files, they can be linked. Alter some figures in Excel and the Word document is immediately updated. Alter the figures in the Word document and the Excel spreadsheet is also updated.

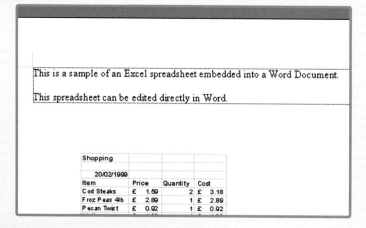

On the left is a screenshot of a picture in Windows Paint – the graphics application that comes with Windows.

This picture was selected in Paint from the Edit menu and Select All. Then, again from the Edit menu Copy was selected (see 'Speed Tip' below). This put the picture on the Clipboard; it was then pasted electronically into the Word document below. This is done within Word by going to Word's Edit menu and choosing Paste.

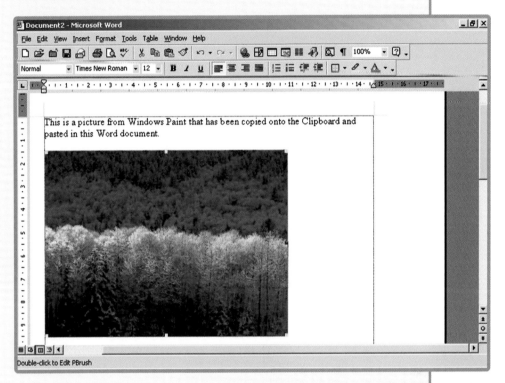

It is worth knowing that the Paint picture is placed in Word as an 'object'. If you click in the middle of this object, little 'handles' appear on the four corners. If you put your mouse pointer over one of these handles, it turns into a double-sided arrow like this.

Click and hold the left mouse button and try dragging the double-sided arrow diagonally from top left to bottom right. This allows you to resize the graphic.

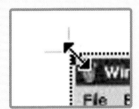

Speed tip

In many applications you can use a combination of keystrokes instead of the mouse — e.g. Ctrl + C to copy a selected portion and Ctrl + V to paste a previously copied item.

TIPS AND TRICKS

Windows is a powerful and complex program, and many large books are devoted to explaining how it works. Just to start you off, here are a handful of tips and tricks that can make using your PC easier.

• Use Help in Windows and all applications.
• Use shortcut keys. Below are some examples.

You can use the following keyboard shortcuts with a Microsoft Natural Keyboard or any other compatible keyboard that includes the Windows logo key (⊞) and the Application key (▤).

Press	To
⊞	Display or hide the **Start** menu.
⊞ +BREAK	Display the **System Properties** dialog box.
⊞ +D	Show the desktop.
⊞ +M	Minimize all windows.
⊞ +Shift+M	Restores minimized windows.
⊞ +E	Open My Computer.
⊞ +F	Search for a file or folder.
CTRL+ ⊞ +F	Search for computers.
⊞ +F1	Display Windows Help.
⊞ + L	Lock your computer if you are connected to a network domain, or switch users if you are not connected to a network domain.
⊞ +R	Open the **Run** dialog box.
▤	Display the shortcut menu for the selected item.
⊞ +U	Open Utility Manager.

- Explore the Windows XP Home Page: www.microsoft.com/windowsxp/home/

- If you are running Windows ME, go here: www.microsoft.com/windowsme/default.asp

- For Windows 98 users, this is the link: www.microsoft.com/windows98/default.asp

- Back up often – at least the important documents and files.

- In Windows XP, set up separate accounts for every active user – as long as you have 64Mb RAM for each person.

- Organise your documents in subject folders.

General keyboard shortcuts

Press	To
CTRL+C	Copy.
CTRL+X	Cut.
CTRL+V	Paste.
CTRL+Z	Undo.
DELETE	Delete.
SHIFT+DELETE	Delete selected item permanently without placing the item in the Recycle Bin.
CTRL while dragging an item	Copy selected item.
CTRL+SHIFT while dragging an item	Create shortcut to selected item.
F2	Rename selected item.
CTRL+RIGHT ARROW	Move the insertion point to the beginning of the next word.
CTRL+LEFT ARROW	Move the insertion point to the beginning of the previous word.
CTRL+DOWN ARROW	Move the insertion point to the beginning of the next paragraph.
CTRL+UP ARROW	Move the insertion point to the beginning of the previous paragraph.
CTRL+SHIFT with any of the arrow keys	Highlight a block of text.
SHIFT with any of the arrow keys	Select more than one item in a window or on the desktop, or select text within a document.
CTRL+A	Select all.
F3	Search for a file or folder.
ALT+ENTER	View properties for the selected item.
ALT+F4	Close the active item, or quit the active program.
ALT+Enter	Displays the properties of the selected object.
ALT+SPACEBAR	Opens the shortcut menu for the active window.
CTRL+F4	Close the active document in programs that allow you to have multiple documents open simultaneously.
ALT+TAB	Switch between open items.
ALT+ESC	Cycle through items in the order they were opened.
F6	Cycle through screen elements in a window or on the desktop.
F4	Display the Address bar list in My Computer or Windows Explorer.
SHIFT+F10	Display the shortcut menu for the selected item.
ALT+SPACEBAR	Display the System menu for the active window.
CTRL+ESC	Display the **Start** menu.
ALT+Underlined letter in a menu name	Display the corresponding menu.
Underlined letter in a command name on an open menu	Carry out the corresponding command.
F10	Activate the menu bar in the active program.
RIGHT ARROW	Open the next menu to the right, or open a submenu.
LEFT ARROW	Open the next menu to the left, or close a submenu.
F5	Refresh the active window.
BACKSPACE	View the folder one level up in My Computer or Windows Explorer.
ESC	Cancel the current task.
SHIFT when you insert a CD into the CD-ROM drive	Prevent the CD from automatically playing.

DIFFERENCES BETWEEN XP AND OLDER VERSIONS OF WINDOWS

This book focuses largely on Windows XP, which was released in October 2001. Virtually all new PCs sold since then have XP (either the Home Edition or the Professional version) installed. If you bought your PC before October 2001, or have recently acquired a second-hand PC, it is likely that it came with Windows 98, ME or possibly 2000. This book does not really cover Windows 95 as that became officially obsolete in November 2001.

There are six main differences between XP and the older versions of Windows.

1. If you upgrade to Windows XP you have to activate XP by telephoning the number given or visiting the website. If you do not activate it, XP will run for only 30 days. Note that this does not apply if you buy a new PC with XP already installed.

2. Windows XP comes from the Windows NT and Windows 2000 family, which is built on much more reliable and robust code than earlier versions. This reliability was first demonstrated in versions of Windows NT4, greatly enhanced in Windows 2000 and brought to fruition in Windows XP. Windows 95, 98 and Windows ME all belong to one family. The key weakness in that family was its reliance on 16-bit code that tried to be compatible with so-called legacy programs (i.e. older versions of software). In addition, Microsoft has made strenuous efforts, first in Windows 2000 and latterly in XP, to debug its code and ensure that things worked from the moment a machine is taken out of its packaging. All the evidence suggests quite strongly that it has succeeded in these aims.

3. XP is strong on security. It forces users to log on; the use of passwords can be enforced.

4. Hardware is the next big difference. You can run Windows 95, 98 and ME on a relatively low-spec PC: you could have a Pentium P166Mhz with 16Mb or 32Mb RAM and a hard disk of 2Gb, and Windows will chug along quite happily. But with XP, you need a more powerful PC. The key difference is the need for a biggish hard disk (at least 10Gb) and a lot of RAM – 128Mb is the bare minimum. Fortunately, in the six years since Windows 95 was released, hardware has become very much cheaper and has increased vastly in power. It is difficult to buy a new PC today whose processor is not powerful enough or

whose hard disk is too small. The only issue you really need to be aware of is the amount of RAM you order with the PC.

5. Software comes next on the list. If you are a fan of Microsoft Office, note that the latest version, Office XP, will not run on Windows 95, no matter how much RAM you have. The positive point is that XP handles older, legacy applications much more effectively. There appear to be a small number of games which are problematic, but no more than with the earlier versions of Windows.

6. Finally, the 'look and feel' of XP is very different from earlier versions. Fortunately, if you are wedded to the 'classic' appearance of previous versions, you can make XP look old.

In addition to the key differences mentioned above, there is an emphasis within XP on multimedia which is not present in earlier versions. Two folders, 'My Music' and 'My Pictures', reflect the thrust within XP towards providing users with programs that play audio and manage a music collection, provide video-editing tools and capture and organise pictures. Windows XP is the first version that really reflects the rapid growth in the use of digital cameras, both still and video.

What has not changed

If you ignore the colours (which you can change anyway), a lot within Windows XP is the same – especially the built-in applications. So, if you have used Windows 95, 98 or ME, you will find that the following facilities are still there:

- Notepad
- WordPad
- Windows Explorer
- Paint
- Control Panel
- various games (including Solitaire!)
- calculator
- Disk Defragmenter
- Scandisk.

Some of the processes remain the same, especially those of installing and removing programs. There is still a desktop, and both My Computer and My Documents have survived the change. So, if you have some experience of older versions of Windows, XP is friendly enough for you to get to grips with its new facilities.

If you are completely new to using a PC and to Windows XP, there is no better place to start than by clicking on **'Start'**, **'All Programs'**, **'Accessories'** and **'Tour Windows XP'**.

Every PC user has different requirements. Although some applications such as word processing and surfing the Internet are very common, arranging the computer's interface to suit your needs and your style can help your productivity. Windows has been designed to be highly capable of customisation.

Changes you can make range from simple (altering colour schemes, say) to complex, such as making Windows perform many tasks automatically. Windows XP allows a user to customise the appearance of Windows extensively. If there are multiple users accessing one PC, each person can customise his or her own account without interfering with the settings of other users.

Customising your machine will help to familiarise you with Windows operations. Experimenting with menus and settings will not damage your system, although it is possible that some types of customisation could cause Windows to behave in a strange and disconcerting manner, even if no error has occurred.

Before making any radical changes (especially in earlier versions of Windows), it is as well to make a note of any settings you intend to alter. If the worst happens, just return the settings to their original values.

Windows XP has a most useful facility for the inveterate tinkerer, called **'System Restore'**. The System Restore tool allows you to restore your computer system to a previous state. This is not only very useful for those who cannot resist fiddling, it is invaluable when a new installation of either software or hardware goes wrong. There is also a version of System Restore in Windows ME.

CUSTOMISING YOUR PC

3.1 **Customising the desktop**
How to create your own, personal desktop

3.2 **Screen properties**
How to change the way Windows works with your monitor

3.3 **Windows Schemes and Themes**
Changing colours, sounds and the look of
Windows using Schemes

3.4 **Multiple users (I)**
Managing multiple users in Windows XP

3.5 **Multiple users (II)**
More tips for managing multiple users

3.6 **Scheduling activities (I)**
Controlling how and when activities are performed

3.7 **Scheduling activities (II)**
Further advice on controlling key events

3.8 **Power management**
How to reduce your PC's energy consumption

3.9 **Accessibility options**
Features for visually and aurally impaired users

3.10 **Making your PC kid-safe**
Tips for setting up your PC, including Internet
safeguards, so that children can use it

CUSTOMISING THE DESKTOP

The Windows desktop is the main interface for accessing features of your PC. It consists of icons that represent links (or shortcuts) to programs or files. Many aspects of the desktop can be personalised (or 'customised') to allow you to have the look you prefer. In Windows XP this customisation has been greatly extended to integrate the Internet. XP allows you to instantly transfer pictures you find when browsing the Net on to your desktop.

If you find a picture or image you like, let your mouse pointer hover over the image and a little menu will pop up. The four options are **'Save this image'**, **'Print this image'**, **'Send this image in an email'** and **'Open My Pictures folder'**. If you right-click in the middle of the picture, another menu (see left) will pop up.

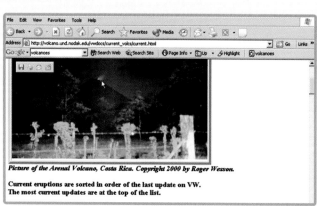

Icons

By pressing the right mouse button over an icon or folder and holding it down, you can drag the item to anywhere on the screen. Make sure that the **'Auto Arrange'** feature (see right) is turned off, otherwise Windows will move the icons to where it believes they should be.

Taskbar properties

Right-click in an empty area of the taskbar and select '**Properties**' to change how it behaves in Windows XP.

'Lock the Taskbar' allows you to lock the taskbar so that it cannot be moved to another edge of the screen.

'Auto hide' removes the taskbar if an application is running, giving more space to the application.

'Keep the Taskbar on top' places the taskbar in front of any running

software, and is very much a matter of personal preference.

'Group similar Taskbar buttons' is very useful for Word users who have several documents open at once.

Arranging icons

The icons on the desktop can be arranged in many different ways. Right-click on the desktop and select '**Arrange Icons**'. From this menu option, you can arrange the icons by name, type, size or date. The '**Auto Arrange**' function allows Windows to control how icons are displayed.

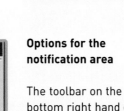

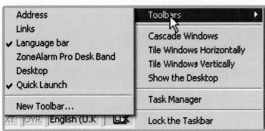

Options for the notification area

The toolbar on the bottom right hand of the desktop, also called the notification area, can be permanently displayed along with Windows applications. This area (like the '**Start**' menu) acts as a convenient way of accessing commonly used features. Right-clicking in the notification area allows you to choose the various options including '**Toolbars**'.

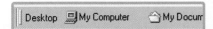

With the '**Links**' option enabled, any website address added to the '**Favorites**' shortcut within the browser (see section 7.2) will be displayed along the toolbar.

With the '**Desktop**' option enabled, every item on the desktop will be replicated in a bar that can scroll from left to right along the toolbar.

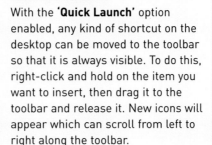

With the '**Quick Launch**' option enabled, any kind of shortcut on the desktop can be moved to the toolbar so that it is always visible. To do this, right-click and hold on the item you want to insert, then drag it to the toolbar and release it. New icons will appear which can scroll from left to right along the toolbar.

More customisation

Each of the different elements of the toolbar, such as 'Address', 'Links', 'Desktop' and 'Quick Launch', can be moved around the toolbar and resized. In fact, the toolbar itself can be resized and moved to different positions around the screen. To resize an element, hold down the left mouse button on an element's description, e.g. the 'Links' button, and move it around. If you hold it on the edge you can resize the item, and if you hold it in the middle you can move it. The same is true of the toolbar itself. Play around with the desktop to see how much you can – and want to – customise it.

SCREEN PROPERTIES

A PC monitor is more adaptable than a television screen in that you can vary many of its features, including the image size and colour capacity. Depending on what kind of task you are performing, you can customise how your monitor displays items – e.g. if you are working with graphics, you can increase the resolution and colour depth. This section explains some of the screen properties you can customise.

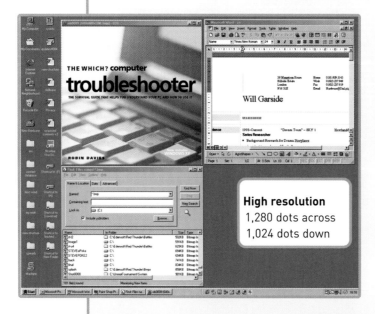

High resolution
1,280 dots across
1,024 dots down

Low resolution
640 dots across
480 dots down
256 colours

The resolution of the screen – i.e. how many dots across and how many dots down can be displayed at any one time – increases with the size of the screen. This resolution figure also includes an indication of the maximum number of colours each dot can display.

These two screens show the difference between high- and low-resolution modes. The high-resolution screen (top) allows more information to be displayed, and with much more detail and richness of colour, than the low-resolution one (below). On the screen below, very little of each application can be seen, and the colours look odd. Having at least 4Mb of memory on your graphics card and a large screen (17 inches or over) enables you to obtain a high-resolution screen.

Changing screen properties

To change the features of your screen, right-click in the Windows desktop area and select **'Properties'**.

1 The **'Background'** tab allows you to select different pictures for your desktop background.

2 The **'Screen Saver'** tab allows you to set up a colour screen saver that will start automatically if your PC is left unattended for long.

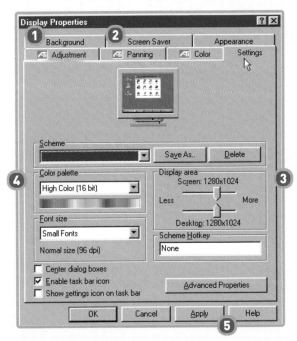

3 The two **'Display area'** sliders affect the resolution of the screen and also how much is displayed at any one time. You can have e.g. a desktop of 1,280 x 1,024 but set your screen size to 800 x 600. With these settings, when the mouse reaches the edge of the visible area the screen scrolls to show the rest of the desktop. This feature is sometimes used in conjunction with large fonts to help visually impaired users.

4 The **'Color palette'** can be varied between 8 bit (256 colours) and 32 bit (16 million) colours. The former is sometimes used with older programs or to improve the PC's performance (the fewer colours it has to manipulate the better it performs),

while the latter is preferred for work with graphics or the manipulation of photographic images.

5 The **'Apply'** button activates any setting you have changed within the **'Display Properties'** section.

Screen savers

The screen saver was created to stop monitors burning out when they displayed the same static image for a long time. Modern monitor design has eliminated this problem. In Windows 95, 98 and ME a password can be set in a screen saver to provide some basic security. However, this can be bypassed quite easily by pressing a PC's reset button and forcing a restart without the screen saver. In Windows 2000 and XP, the weakness has been overcome as both versions offer rigorous, password-protected security (where implemented).

WINDOWS SCHEMES AND THEMES

With the help of Display Properties you can make a whole variety of changes to the way Windows XP looks in order to make your account as individual as you wish.

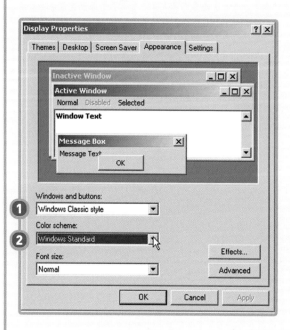

Selecting and using Windows Schemes and Themes

In order to select and use Schemes, right-click on the Windows desktop and select **'Properties'**. In the **'Display Properties'** dialog box select the **'Appearance'** tab and you are presented with the following options.

1 If you click on the **'Windows and buttons'** drop-down dialog box, you are presented with a list of ready-made options for colours and font sizes. These schemes have names such as 'rose' and 'storm'. If you click on, say, rose, the colour of the dialog boxes will turn from the Windows standard blue to a pink.

2 If you click on the **'Color Schemes'** drop-down box, you are presented with more options (see left) to customise individual items. You can e.g. change the size and colour scheme of a message box or the scroll bar.

Changing and exploring sounds

Many events and occurrences in
Windows are accompanied by
sounds. You can, if you wish, vary the
default settings either to turn off the
sounds or to change them.

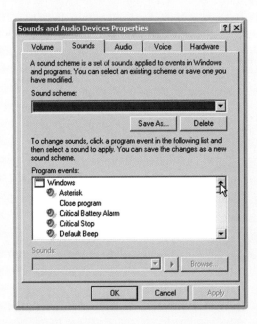

To test or change the sounds used by your PC,
select the **'Sound and Audio Devices Properties'**
icon in the Control Panel (click on **'Start'** and then
'Settings'). You can preview various sounds by
using the play and stop buttons. You can assign
different sounds to different events and save this
information as your own personal scheme. Simply
select an event which defines a particular action
being carried out (e.g. exiting Windows) and then
assign a sound you would like to hear when that
event occurs.

MULTIPLE USERS (I)

For the first time in releases of Windows aimed at home users, Windows XP enforces the use of accounts and provides real security. This section explains the basics of user accounts (multiple users) under XP. Windows XP has built on the high levels of user security which first appeared in Windows NT and which were taken further in Windows 2000 (which was primarily for business users on a network).

As with earlier versions, XP should start automatically when you switch on your PC. The first thing you will see is this.

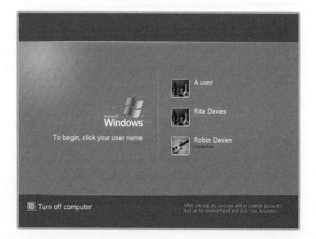

RAM requirements

XP eats RAM when you have multiple users on a PC. You will require 64Mb for each user account that is open. A family of four users, each with a separate account open, would need a PC with 256Mb of RAM. At the time of writing, a 256Mb stick of suitable RAM for most PCs can be purchased for about £60.

Here you see three accounts created. XP allows three kinds of accounts to be set up:
- administrator
- limited
- guest.

An **administrator** account (which is automatically created when XP is first installed) can create all new accounts and allows changes to these accounts.

A **limited** account allows a user to change his or her own settings (altering the display and general layout of the desktop) and to access the parts of Windows XP that the administrator permits.

A **guest** account can run some programs and may have limited data file access. It cannot access any key system files and is a pretty restricted account.

Important: password for administrator account

In a PC that has several user accounts, the administrator that is automatically created when XP is installed (or is there when you first start a new PC provided with XP) should be set with a secure password. The administrator account is all-powerful and can create, alter or remove other accounts. If you are in a family situation and want to exercise some control over your errant children, this password is vital.

Why have accounts?

If you live by yourself, the only account on an XP-based computer will be yours and it will be one with administrator permissions. However, even in that situation you should set a strong password. If you have sensitive information on your PC, password-protecting the account becomes important. If other people use the PC as well as you, you will find that Windows XP offers the ideal way to provide each user with an individual and secure working environment.

The perfect family or multiple-user PC is one in which everybody can organise their own Windows desktop, schemes, colours and sounds which appears when they log on, but is not altered by anybody else. Parents can have their own accounts, secure in the knowledge that the kids have theirs, and that the bizarre games, sounds and colours they prefer do not impact upon what the parents do!

With XP, it is even easy and safe to log off your account and let somebody else log on for up to 20 minutes. When the other user logs off and you come back and log on, you will find all your documents still available.

Passwords

Passwords need to be **'strong'**. Do not use anything obvious, such as the name of your partner, the cat or the goldfish, or birth dates or telephone numbers. Do use a mixture of letters and numbers and make one of the letters upper-case (capital). One last point, sticking a note on the monitor with your password on is not very secure!

3 | Customising your PC

MULTIPLE USERS (II)

Setting up accounts

Click on **'Start'** and choose **'Control Panel'**.

Then select **'User Accounts'**.

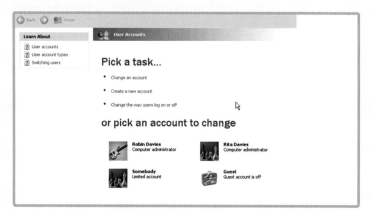

This allows you to maintain accounts, including creating new ones.

The next step is to decide what permissions to grant – and it is normally a choice between **'computer administrator'** and **'limited'**. For the reasons outlined in Section 3.4, all new accounts should be limited accounts.

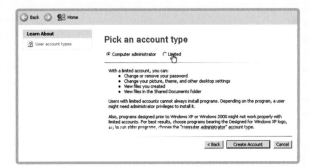

Having selected the account type, you then create the account. The **'User Accounts'** option in the Control Panel allows you to manage the accounts and change various settings.

The Help and Support option in the Start menu is a useful resource for this topic (and all other aspects of Windows XP).

Summary

- Windows XP, unlike Windows 95, 98 or ME, requires all users to log on.
- The basic starter account in XP has administrator permissions and should be password-protected.
- Where there are multiple users, each person should have his or her own account.

- You need 64Mb of RAM for each account open.
- Passwords should be 'strong': avoid the obvious.

XP supports 'Fast User Switching' of accounts, allowing more than one account to be open at a time, subject to the memory requirements mentioned above.

SCHEDULING ACTIVITIES (I)

What to schedule and when

You can set up many different types of tasks for the Scheduler to perform. The wizard in the 'Scheduled Tasks' utility lists the options you can choose from depending on the software installed on your machine. Common tasks include Scandisk, disk defragmentation, disk cleanup and backing up important files.

Some important computer housekeeping activities can be easily forgotten. Surfing the Net, playing a game or even doing the household accounts can be much more interesting. Perhaps it is a bit like painting the outside of the house: very important but conveniently forgotten. Windows XP has a useful utility called Scheduled Tasks which can automate the running of any program at a time to suit you and the PC.

How to schedule activities

In order to run schedule activities click on **'Start'**, **'Control Panel'** and **'Performance and Maintenance'**.

Choose **'Scheduled Tasks'**.

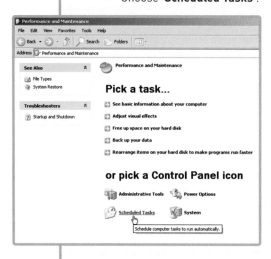

This launches you into the Scheduled Task Wizard which will walk you through the process.

Windows XP offers you a list of programs which can be scheduled, but you can also add others by selecting **'Browse'** and picking a program.

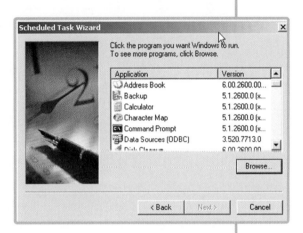

Once you choose the program to add to the task scheduler (in the example below **'Disk Cleanup'**), you are asked to give a name to the task and specify how often you would like it to be run.

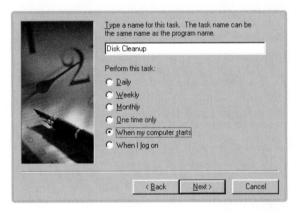

After the Wizard guides you through the entire process of setting up a scheduled task, you are prompted by a dialog box which confirms all the options you have chosen.

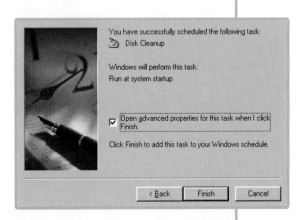

SCHEDULING ACTIVITIES (II)

The Scheduled Tasks Wizard automatically offers you a selection of programs to schedule and suggests that you can browse to the programs you wish to schedule. However, in practice that is not as straightforward as the Wizard suggests. This is, unfortunately, particularly true in the Windows XP versions. You might, for instance, wish to automatically schedule disk defragmentation once a month. Using the '**Browse**' option in the Wizard to do this is convoluted.

There is a rather easier way – put a shortcut on the desktop first (see below) and just drag and drop (with the mouse) the shortcut icon into the Scheduler window.

Creating a program shortcut on the desktop

There are three ways to create a desktop shortcut. One way is to click on '**Start**' and '**Help and Support**' and work your way from '**Customizing your Computer**'. Start with '**Your Desktop**' and follow the obvious prompts. At least 11 steps are involved, but the process is clearly set out.

☑ Search only Customizing your computer

Customizing your computer

- ⊡ Your desktop
- ⊡ Your desktop icons
- ⊡ Your Start menu
- ⊡ Background and themes
- ⊡ Screen savers and screen settings
- ☐ Files, folders, and programs
- ⊡ Keyboard and mouse
- ⊡ Multiple monitors
- ⊡ Fonts and text

See Also

- ? Windows Glossary
- ? Windows keyboard shortcuts overview
- ? Tools
- ? Go to a Windows newsgroup

To use the second method, start by right-clicking in an empty area of the desktop and select '**New**' and '**Shortcut**'.

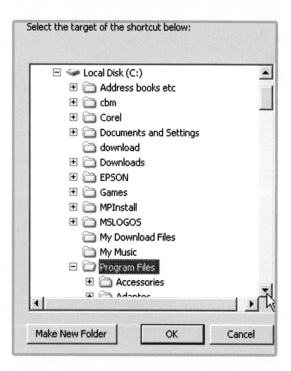

Select the target of the shortcut below:

⊟ 💾 Local Disk (C:)
  ⊞ 📁 Address books etc
  ⊞ 📁 cbm
  ⊞ 📁 Corel
  ⊞ 📁 Documents and Settings
    📁 download
  ⊞ 📁 Downloads
  ⊞ 📁 EPSON
  ⊞ 📁 Games
  ⊞ 📁 MPInstall
  ⊞ 📁 MSLOGOS
    📁 My Download Files
    📁 My Music
  ⊟ 📁 Program Files
    ⊞ 📁 Accessories
    ⊞ 📁 Adapter

Make New Folder | OK | Cancel

Then browse to the
program you require
(usually in C:\Program
Files) as follows.

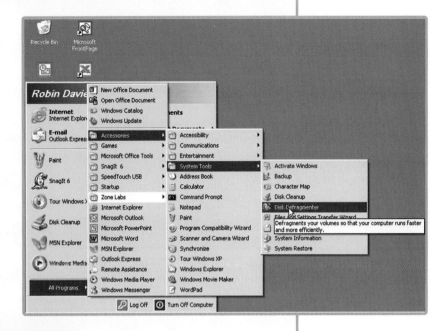

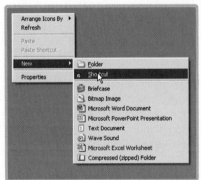

About the same number of steps is
involved as in the first method, but
experienced users find it very quick.

The third way is just to use the
mouse to drag and drop the program
icon from the Start menu on to the
desktop.

Once you are accustomed to using the mouse to
drag and drop, this can be a very fast method.
Practise often and do not be afraid to delete any
icons you create. You do not delete a program
when you delete a desktop shortcut.

Once the icon is on the desktop, you can just
drag and drop it into the Scheduler window.

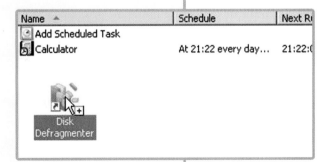

POWER MANAGEMENT

Power Options

Modern PCs are designed to be left on permanently. However, like a video recorder, when a PC is not in use it can automatically go into a sleep mode that draws less electricity. This section explains the fundamentals of power management and how to configure your system for standby mode.

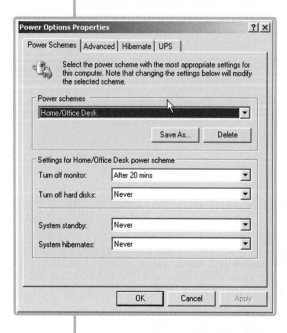

Using power management tools

Controlling the electricity consumption of your PC is essential from an environmental point of view. To do so, select the **'Power Options'** icon that can be found in the Control Panel. You can then customise various key settings on your computer which cater to your individual needs and usage (e.g. if you have to leave your PC on to receive faxes but are not using the system, you can set up Power Management schemes that will save electricity consumption).

Modern monitors tend to use a lot of electricity. You can manually set the period of inactivity which automatically turns your monitor to a low-power 'standby' mode.

The best power management for a monitor may well be to turn it off (but leave the PC on) if you intend not to use it for a long time. The only danger is that another user may think that your PC is actually off and in trying to switch it 'on' actually turns it off, thus perhaps causing damage.

Advanced Power Management

If you click on the **'Advanced'** tab you can choose to display a power icon in the taskbar. This can be especially useful for laptop users, so they can gauge how much power is left in the battery pack. You can also set up an option to have the computer ask for a password when you want to get into the system after it has been in standby mode. This prevents other people from accessing your PC and account without permission.

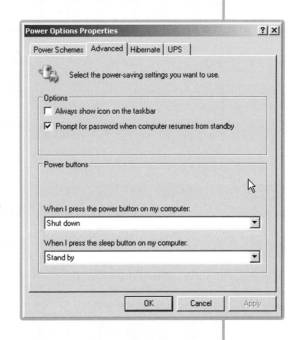

UPS settings

If you have a UPS (uninterruptible power supply) the **'UPS'** tab allows you to select and configure the UPS device.

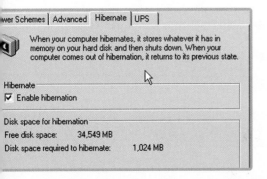

Hibernation

If you have set your PC to hibernate through the **'Power Schemes'** tab (see screengrab on facing page), you will also need to check the **'Enable hibernation'** box on the **'Hibernate'** tab. This tab also shows if you have enough disk space available for hibernation to occur.

ACCESSIBILITY OPTIONS

The 'Accessibility Options' feature in Windows provides help for users who have sight or hearing impairments or limited dexterity. They can choose to have, say, large fonts, visual cues replacing audio cues, or adapted keyboards. This section looks at how to configure Accessibility Options.

To change Accessibility Options, click on **'Start'**, **'Control Panel'** and then the **'Accessibility Options'** icon.

The keyboard options are useful for people who have limited dexterity.

The **'StickyKeys'** feature removes the need to hold down special keys such as Ctrl or Alt while typing another character. Usually, to copy data you hold Ctrl and press C; with **'StickyKeys'** you press Ctrl first, then C separately, to achieve the same thing.

If you have difficulty typing and tend to hold keys down longer than necessary, you can make Windows ignore the extra keystrokes by using the **'FilterKeys'** option.

More information

For more information on Accessibility Options in Windows, click on the **'Start'** menu and select **'Help'**. At the prompt, type in **'Accessibility'**, and then double-click on any entries you want to explore further.

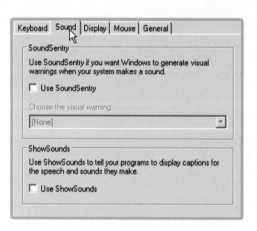

The **'Sound'** options replace audio cues with visual ones and *vice versa*. These options work in some applications.

With the **'High Contrast'** mode activated, Windows looks like the example on the right. This mode is helpful for partially sighted users.

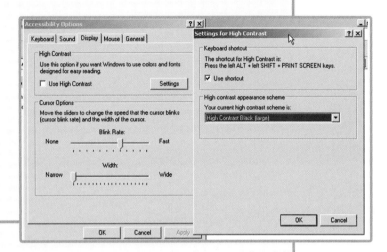

The **'Mouse'** option allows you to use the keyboard or numeric keypad instead of the mouse.

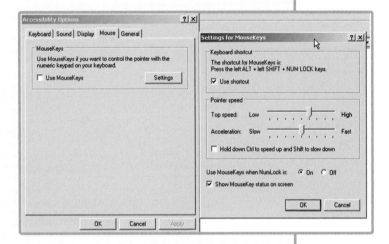

The **'General'** tab covers other useful Accessibility Options such as audio warnings when features are turned on and off. At the bottom of the **'General'** tab are two settings which allow the administrator of the PC (see section 3.4) to configure the implementation of these accessibility settings for users in general.

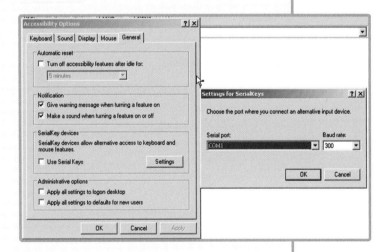

MAKING YOUR PC KID-SAFE

Warning!

Children should not be left unsupervised with an Internet connection. Avoid putting a PC in a child's bedroom where he or she can shut the door so you do not know what is going on. Computers are inherently hackable, and most of the restrictions you impose on your offspring's Internet usage can, unfortunately, be circumvented. Education is often the best form of protection.

The PC can be a great way for children to learn and to communicate with others, especially by using the Internet. However, there are parts of the Internet where they can be exposed to pornography, foul language or the activities of undesirable people. Although the PC itself is resilient to children altering its settings, particularly under Windows XP, concerned adults should learn how to help kids enjoy using the PC while minimising the risks.

Protecting important files

The first – and most vital – step is to use Windows XP to create individual accounts (see section 3.4) accessible only by password. Make your children's accounts 'limited' when you set them up. This enables you to restrict access in any way you feel is appropriate without spoiling effective use. As a parent, remember that you are the PC's administrator and your account under XP must be password-protected and that password kept secure from other users. You can buy software called 'Childlock', which stops your children from accessing certain areas of your PC.

Making the Internet safe for your children

Although some Internet service providers (ISPs) now offer special areas, sometimes called 'walled gardens', which are deemed safe for children, many do not, and you will need to look for alternatives. Take the following steps to maximise your children's safety on the Net.

• Place the PC in an easily accessible area, not in a bedroom. Think twice before allowing your child to use the PC in a room with the door shut.
• With older pre-teens and teens talk honestly about the dangers and set ground rules. Accept that if your child visits a friend's home, he or she may have access to the Internet without any restrictions. That is why education is a good policy.
• Consider buying programs such as Net Nanny or Cyber Patrol. Such software costs about £35. N2H2 and Weblocker (free) are to be recommended too. However, they are not 100% effective.
• Visit sites such as www.safekids.com and www.microsoft.com/privacy/safeinternet/topics/children.htm.

There is a possibility of real danger through encounters made in online chat rooms, but it happens very rarely and can be avoided by following the steps listed above.

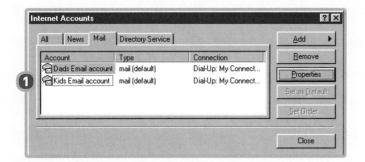

Screening email

Tremendous fun can be had from sending and receiving email. For many children, sending email from school to other students in schools around the world is a useful way of finding out more about life in other countries. They will want to do this at home. Even when they grow up and leave home, they will find email useful, as a way of keeping in touch with parents, relatives and friends in other parts of the world. Sadly, in recent years there has been a rise in the number of junk emails, called 'spam'. Most email clients allow you to set filters to delete such junk email but, again, they are not fully effective.

When you create settings for your children to use email, make sure that you leave out any personal information from email signatures. Users' names and postal addresses should never be sent in email used by children. One exception might be to a known school email address.

You can also set up your email so that you can access your child's email account from your own.

1 Create a new connection in your email program using your children's email details.

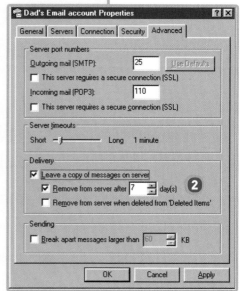

2 Change both your own and your children's advanced settings so that email messages are not removed from your ISP's server for at least seven days.

Now when you log on all your email and your children's email will be downloaded into your email inbox.

Note that if you have older pre-teens and teenage children who use the PC, you will need to discuss with them the best way of using email safely and wisely. Under Windows XP you will have created their individual accounts and passwords. This will allow you to log on to their accounts if you have any worries about the nature of the emails your children are sending or receiving.

Physical protection for your PC

To stop children opening up your PC you can fit security screws that require a specially shaped key to undo them.
   You can also buy a special lock for the floppy drive and remove the CD-ROM drive from the BIOS to prevent children from installing software without your knowledge.

3 | Customising your PC

Many complex tasks go on inside a modern PC. As the power of computers and the demands we make of them grow, so too do opportunities for hardware- and software-related problems.

Fortunately, with XP, Windows has become much more reliable. You are more likely to have problems with peripherals, such as printers and scanners, as well as programs that require powerful graphics.

Every Windows program has a help file built into it (accessed by pressing F1) and you may even have a manual provided. For most popular applications you can also find much help on the Internet and in books.

In this section we look at some of the most common problems faced by users and offer advice on how to deal with them.

BASIC TROUBLESHOOTING

4 | Basic troubleshooting

FAULT OR QUIRK OF WINDOWS?

Sometimes Windows may appear to be behaving oddly, but is often just performing a housekeeping task or demonstrating a feature. Before re-installing software, or opening up the case and ripping out hardware, you need to determine whether the problem is actually a fault or just a quirk of Windows. To diagnose faults you need to know about common Windows operations which can otherwise appear to be errors.

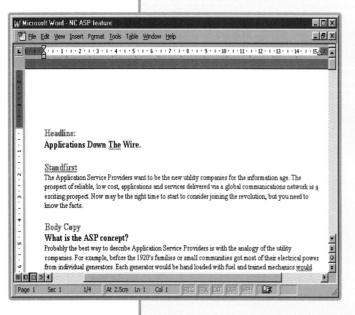

Missing toolbar

In the example to the left toolbars have been turned off. This can occur if you select the wrong menu option or press the wrong key combination. The toolbars can easily be restored if you look at the View menu and select **'Toolbars'**. Just select the ones you want to see (the defaults are to show Standard and Formatting).

Character overwriting when typing

Usually if the cursor is placed within the middle of a sentence and you start typing, the remainder of the sentence gets pushed along by the text you type. If you see each character you type replacing the existing text, character by character, you have pressed the Insert key by accident. This key changes the text mode from the usual one of Insert to a mode called Overtype. Press the **'Insert'** key again to return things to normal.

Number pad not working

Are strange things happening when you try to type in numbers from the keypad? Does the cursor jump around the page at random? Are characters being deleted? Check the lights on the keyboard, particularly the NumLock light and Scroll Lock. The chances are that these have been turned on/off and the keys have taken on an entirely different function.

Files start oddly

Sometimes double-clicking on a document just does not do what you expect. It may activate a different application, or Windows may ask you for the name of the application with which it should open the file. The cause may be a change in the program/document relationship. When you double-click a document saved, say, in Word, Windows makes sure that Word is the program it uses to re-open the document. Most applications use a file-name suffix to indicate this, e.g. .DOC for Microsoft Word, .XLS for Microsoft Excel or .BMP (bitmap) for graphics programs. A newly installed application may try to take over the association with a particular file format. Within the preferences of any new software you may see options for file associations under the guise of extensions, usually under an Options menu choice or sometimes under Preferences. File associations can be altered manually via the Folder Options menu on any Windows Explorer window (click on the File Types tab). See File Types at the back of the book.

Turning on features

Quite often, odd behaviour in Windows or one of its many applications results from an obscure feature being turned on accidentally. Sometimes, the application's Help file can provide the answer (see example opposite, from within Word, with the disappearing toolbars). In the Toolbar's Help menu, under Contents, you can type **'displaying'** or **'hiding'**, which are in the list of topics: this can be a good place to start if you encounter this kind of problem.

TESTING YOUR PC

Power-on testing

The most likely time for a PC to break down is while it is starting up (booting). The computer runs a series of tests on each piece of hardware before loading the operating system. If a device fails the Power-On-Self-Test (POST), it may cause the machine to stop the booting procedure. The POST normally shows messages that say which devices have passed testing and which have failed.

Common causes of PC problems are loose or faulty connections between external devices and the main system unit. Good troubleshooting practice is to check all the connections and peripherals before moving on to more advanced troubleshooting.

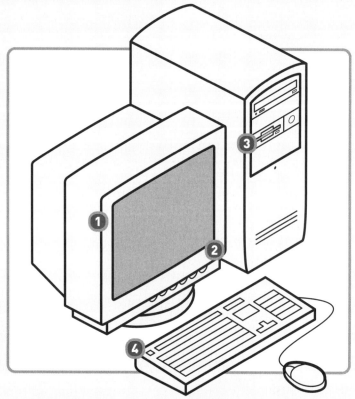

Warning!

To save energy, some computers appear to turn themselves off if left unattended. Pressing the keyboard or mouse starts the computer up again.

Computer fails to start when 'on' button is pressed

1 Check the screen Read any information displayed on the screen. Some systems may require a password or particular key to be depressed before you are allowed to continue.

2 Is the monitor on? Your computer system unit may be working but your monitor may either be off or have suffered a failure. Monitors tend to last 3-5 years.

3 Remove floppy disk If you use a 3¹/₂-inch floppy disk to transfer work, remove it before turning off or starting up your PC.

4 Examine keyboard If a key has been stuck in the 'down' position this can prevent a computer from starting correctly.

5 Check mains power Ensure that the mains is switched on. Use a bedside lamp or clock to test that the plug socket still has power.

6 **Monitor connection** A 15-pin cable connects your monitor to the system unit. Ensure that the cable is connected. The plug will only go in one way so do not force anything that seems tight.

7 **Power to system unit** A three-wire power cable normally runs from the mains to the system unit. Many PCs also have a power cable that runs from the system unit to the monitor. Ensure that this is not loose.

8 **Peripheral connection** The back of your PC has connections for a mouse and a keyboard. These connectors are very similar in design — round in shape, with six holes. They should be marked for easy identification. If not, finding the right one through trial and error will not damage your PC. The mouse may instead work by a wider nine-pin connector called the serial port. This connection is sometimes used for modems. Most PCs also come with two USB ports which are normally used for printers and scanners.

9 **Device connection** A longer 25-hole connector, called a parallel port, is standard on desktop PCs. This is commonly used for printers and scanners, especially the cheaper models. External storage devices, such as Zip drives, commonly use either the parallel connection or a USB connection.

Bits and PCs

A PC computer system consists of only nine major components. The chance of more than one component failing simultaneously is minuscule.

Protecting the PSU

The PSU (power supply unit) is essentially a transformer, converting mains voltage to the 5, 9 or 12 volts used by your system unit. Irregular mains supply and rare occurrences like lightning or blackouts can damage the PSU and connected computer equipment. A UPS (uninterruptible power supply) or surge protector can help protect vulnerable systems and provide power for a short period in the event of a power cut. A cheaper alternative to a UPS is a surge-resistant extension plug. These come in various sizes, taking up to eight devices and protecting your modem's phone line as well.

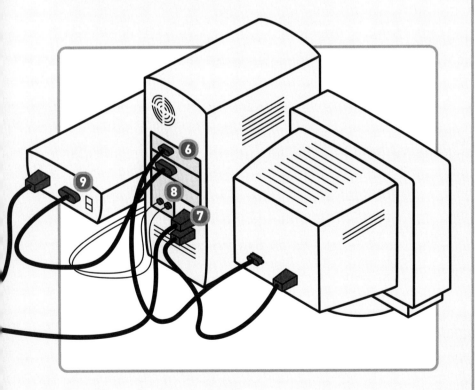

DIAGNOSTIC TOOLS FOR WINDOWS 98

When Windows does have a problem, finding the cause of the error can be time-consuming. All versions of Windows contain tools to help you with problems in your hardware and software, although there are differences between the versions. This section explains some ways of using these tools within Windows 98. See section 4.4 for the differences in Windows ME, 2000 and XP.

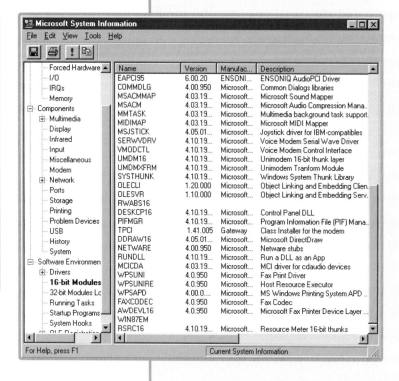

The Microsoft System Information tool comes free with some versions of Windows 98 and with several Microsoft applications. The utility can be found in the c:\Program Files\Common Files\Microsoft shared\msinfo folder under the name Msinfo32.exe. Many of the options and features are very technical; however, the accompanying Help file is very useful.

The msinfo program gives you a detailed description of each application, whether it is running in memory or on the hard disk: the description includes its name, version number, who created the program and what it does. Sometimes an application generates an error message. With msinfo you can find out what the application does and which company created the application so you can contact it for technical support. By having the version number of an application you can look on the manufacturer's website for a newer version of the application if the version you have is producing errors.

1 The Windows Report tool creates a complete analysis of your Windows system (what is running, your default printer, and so on).

2 If you have applied a Windows update which is not working properly, this option removes the update.

3 This tool checks important Windows files for possible corruption.

4 The Signature Verification tool is used mostly by developers, seldom for troubleshooting.

5 The registry contains thousands of individual program settings: this utility checks for errors.

6 This option, for Windows experts only, is used to make the system ignore device drivers at start-up.

7 Dr Watson is a useful utility for monitoring the system and detecting

1	Windows Report Tool
2	Update Wizard Uninstall
3	System File Checker
4	Signature Verification Tool
5	Registry Checker
6	Automatic Skip Driver Agent
7	Dr. Watson
8	System Configuration Utility
9	ScanDisk
10	Version Conflict Manager

errors. It uses a small amount of processor and memory capacity.

8 The System Configuration utility changes the way in which Windows starts up and shuts down. It is inadvisable to alter these settings.

9 See section 2.2.

10 When you install new system drivers, the old versions are often backed up by the system. This utility can restore these older versions if necessary.

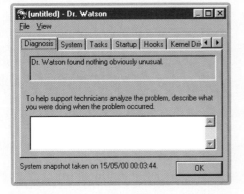

Dr Watson

The Dr Watson utility automatically scans your system for errors. When running, it leaves a small icon in the bottom right-hand corner of the taskbar. If a program crashes, clicking on this icon may help you find out why the error has occurred.

DIAGNOSTIC TOOLS FOR WINDOWS ME, 2000 AND XP

One of the most common problems you are likely to face with Windows is that it sometimes does not start properly. This is usually the result of not shutting Windows down correctly before the power is turned off. Perversely, to shut Windows down you must first click on the **'Start'** icon at the bottom left of your screen.

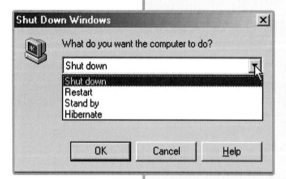

In Windows ME you will see this.

In Windows XP things are different, but you are still faced with some choices.

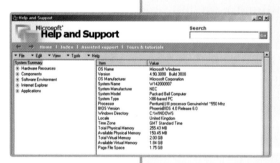

Problems shutting down?

Occasionally, trying to shut Windows down can be troublesome. Both Windows 98 and ME have been known to show shutdown problems when some anti-virus packages are being used. You may need to visit the website of the anti-virus supplier or the Microsoft site for an update to solve any problems.

Section 4.3 referred to the Microsoft System Information tool. In Windows ME, 2000 and XP this tool underwent some changes. However, you still start the tool in the same way. Click on **'Start'**, then **'Run'** and type **'msinfo32'** and press enter or click on **'OK'**. In ME you will see the screen on the left, which is aptly labelled 'Help and Support'.

In Windows XP you will see this (see right).

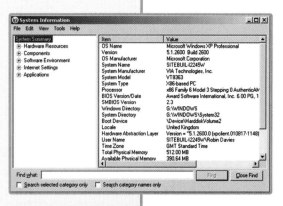

The tools listed in the previous section are a little different in later versions, with the ME version looking like this.

WMI Control
System Restore
Network Diagnostics
DirectX Diagnostic Tool
Update Wizard Uninstall
Signature Verification Tool
Registry Checker
Automatic Skip Driver Agent
Dr Watson
System Configuration Utility
ScanDisk

Help is always on hand

In all versions of Windows there is an option on the Start menu labelled either 'Help' or 'Help and Support'. This large file is very useful and is particularly good in Windows XP.

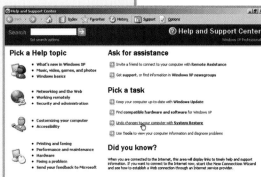

Safe mode

Safe mode is a very useful option when things go wrong and Windows cannot start properly. Most drivers are not loaded and a very basic screen display driver is used. If Windows starts successfully in safe mode, then the most likely cause of problems are faulty drivers. You may have just installed some new hardware or a new game. If, after you uninstall the hardware and related software, Windows boots up correctly, it is more than likely that they were to blame. Always close down all anti-virus software and other applications before installing new hardware and software. For test purposes, it is useful to know how to force a safe mode start-up.

To restart Windows 95 in safe mode
1. Restart the computer.
2. Watch the screen while it is still black. When you see 'Starting Windows 95', immediately press the F8 key. Windows starts in safe mode.

To restart Windows 98 or Windows ME in safe mode
1. Restart the computer.
2. During restart, hold down the Ctrl key until the Startup menu appears.
3. Choose **'safe mode'** from the start-up menu, and press **'Enter'**. Windows starts in safe mode.

In Windows 2000 and XP you have an option to press F8 as part of the start-up process. See section 5.5 for details.

TERMINATING AN ERRANT PROGRAM

Software today is very complex, and some programs – e.g. Windows XP – are huge, with millions of lines of code. Whether or not that is a good thing is beyond the scope of this book. What is beyond doubt is that programs sometimes 'fall over' or 'crash'. The impact of such crashes upon Windows varies considerably. Earlier versions, such as Windows 95, 98 and ME, often just 'died' in the face of badly behaved programs, and getting out of the mess was often difficult. Sometimes the solution was to press three keys – Ctrl-Alt-Del – and then this window would open, which would enable you to terminate a problematic application.

With the advent of Windows 2000, Microsoft made strenuous efforts to reduce the number of times Windows might crash. This improvement has been greatly enhanced with Windows XP, and users have, at last, a very stable version of Windows that handles errant programs effectively.

Nevertheless, there will be occasions when you need to stop a program. In Windows XP pressing Ctrl-Alt-Del will display the Windows 'Task Manager' (which first appeared in Windows NT). Note that in Windows 2000, this does not happen. Instead, you will see a 'Windows Security' screen in which 'Task Manager' is a button you press.

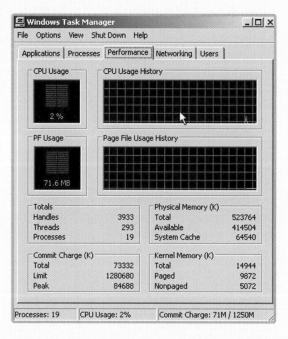

How to use Task Manager

Step 1
Click on the **'Applications'** tab to see which programs are running.

Step 2
If a program is listed as not responding, just select it with one left-click and then click on **'End Task'.** In the vast majority of cases that action will end the program and you can return to Windows normally. In rare cases there will be no response. You may then have to move to Step 3.

Step 3
If a program refuses to end, select the **'Shut Down'** option from the menus at the top and choose to **'Log Off'**, **'Restart'** or **'Switch User'.**

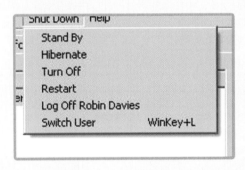

Why do programs crash?

Although modern software is far more reliable than that run on the punchcard-driven computers of the 1970s, most applications will still crash under certain circumstances. The reason may be bad programming within the millions of lines of computer code which make up each program. Sometimes an error occurs when applications try to communicate with each other, possibly because of differences in the versions of the programs: such so-called 'conflicts' are common. However, the most frequent cause of crashes is user interaction. Most software companies actively encourage users to report problems that occur when users find new ways to interact with software, so that the problems can be fixed for subsequent versions.

FIXING APPLICATION ERRORS

Some software applications/programs crash constantly under certain circumstances. All software has relationships with parts of the Windows operating system, hardware devices and other software. Often, to solve an application error, you need to fix the underlying cause of the error. To do this you have to understand the relationships between the applications and how to test each part of Windows to see if it is working correctly.

COMMON PROBLEMS AND POSSIBLE CAUSES

Programs crash unexpectedly

• Try closing any other applications which may be running in the background or on the taskbar, then try running the application again.
• Try restarting Windows, followed by running a full ScanDisk to correct any problems on the hard disk. See section 2.2.

• Remove applications from the Startup group. Restart Windows before testing the errant application again.
• Check the application's manual or help files for a 'known errors' or 'troubleshooting' section.

Program will not start

• Some applications require the original installation CD-ROM to be present in the drive before the application will start (this is an anti-piracy measure).
• Some applications depend on a hardware device being live before they can function correctly. For example, scanning software normally needs the scanner to be activated before the program can start.
• Some applications require the screen resolution and colour depth to be set to the correct values before the software starts (see section 3.2).
• Some older programs work only in DOS.

Application file won't save

• If you try to save a file which is used by another application, Windows may prevent this from happening.
• Some types of files, especially graphics formats, can take up tens of megabytes of space. For example, trying to save an image from a scanner on to a floppy disk is not possible if the image is greater than 1.44Mb in size.
• Files can be locked into a read-only mode by users or other applications. Trying to save a new file with the same name as the locked file may cause an error. Try saving the file with a new name or to a different location on the hard drive.

Application display looks garbled

• Some applications may appear garbled or unreadable. For better results, try changing the screen resolution, as outlined in section 3.2.
• Each application may support many different viewing options. Look for a menu option called 'View' or under 'Options' or 'Preferences'.

Troubleshooting tips

• Check for viruses.
• Use the software help files.
• Look for the 'readme' file for 'known errors'.
• Restart Windows.
• Re-install the application.
• Contact technical support for the application.
• Examine the website of the errant application for technical assistance or a newer version of the software.

Why a menu feature does not work

• Some features such as cut/copy need a piece of text, or other item selected on the screen before they become highlighted.

• If you have a lower-price or demo version of a software package certain advanced features may be disabled, despite appearing on the menu (check the menu's help or version options: telltale words include 'limited edition', 'demo' or 'beta version').

• If you load a file which has been set by another user for viewing only into an application, some of the editing/saving options may have been restricted, to prohibit changes.

• You may need to add additional parts, known as plug-ins, for some features of applications: these are sometimes provided free of charge.

FIXING PRINTER PROBLEMS

Modern printers are generally very reliable and capable of astonishingly accurate photographic reproduction. The inkjet printer unit itself is largely a mechanism for moving the print head and ink cartridges across the paper. The wizardry is in the print head, which is the part of the printer that responds to the software driver and produces the impressive output we all expect. That is the main reason a set of new cartridges can cost a third of the price of an £80 printer. Laser printers are considerably more complicated, but as reliable.

COMMON PROBLEMS AND POSSIBLE CAUSES

Is the printer plugged into the correct socket?
Most modern printers use either the parallel or the USB socket for connection to the PC. Make sure the cable is securely fitted between PC and printer.

Is the paper correctly loaded?
Are the sheets sticking together?
Many basic printers accept up to 100 sheets of paper within the paper feed. You may sometimes need to riffle one corner of a new batch of paper to loosen the sheets before reloading the paper tray.

Has the right paper type been selected within the application?
Printers can accept many sizes of paper. Within the printer options within an application, make sure that the paper size matches the paper loaded into the printer.

Is the print quality poor?
• Check the ink level of the printer cartridges.
• Many printers have a self-cleaning mode (check the manual for how to start this mode).
• Look in the driver options for different 'quality' modes, such as draft, standard and high quality, and select the one you want.
• With ink printers, if one colour fails the printed image may start to look odd, with some colours missing entirely. You may need to replace an ink cartridge.
• The software for many modern inkjet printers has options to clean and adjust the print heads. This can solve some problems.

Is the printer switched on and 'online'?
The printer must be switched on and also turned to 'online'. 'Online' means that it is able to receive data. When a printer is online a small light or other visual indication normally appears. An inkjet printer must be switched off using the on/off button on the printer itself before the mains supply is switched off. This allows the heads to be 'parked' correctly.

Is the printer driver installed and set as the default printer?
Each printer has an associated piece of driving software. Make sure your printer driver is installed and set as the default. Follow the guide on the facing page.

Has the right paper source been selected?
Most printers have a second paper feed for single sheets, such as letterheads. Select which feed (or tray) to use within the printing section of the application.

Setting the default printer

In Windows 98 and ME, the procedure is the same. Click on the **'Start'** menu, select **'Control Panel'**, then select **'Printers'**. From here, right-click on the printer icon which matches your make and model and select **'Set as Default'**.

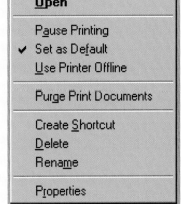

Windows XP assumes, through the installation process, that if you have installed a printer it is going to be the default printer. When running through the Add Printer Wizard, you specify which printer Windows uses as its default. If you install a second printer (perhaps a laser one for extensive black and white printing), you have a choice of which to install as the default.

The Print Dialog Box

When you print from an application, Windows will use the default printer. If you have two printers installed, the default printer will be at the top of the list, but you can scroll down and, if you wish, choose the other printer from the Print Dialog Box.

Note that in many applications, such as Microsoft Word, there is a printer icon which, if clicked, prints the whole document to the default printer. No choice is given. To select printers where more than one is installed, you must print via the File menu.

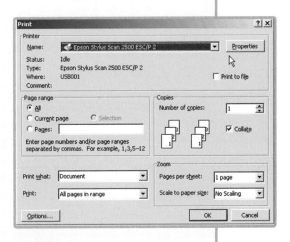

FIXING SCANNER PROBLEMS

The optical scanner takes paper-based images and converts them into digital images. A scanner connects to a PC by the parallel port, the USB port or a SCSI interface, and there are several methods of controlling the internal electronics for scanning and transferring data to the PC. Even though scanners vary between manufacturers, taking some simple troubleshooting steps can solve many of the common problems.

COMMON PROBLEMS AND POSSIBLE CAUSES

Is the scanner plugged into the computer?
Check all the connections between the PC and the scanner.

If the scanner is connected via the printer, are both devices switched on?
Many older scanners use the printer port for scanning. You need to ensure that both devices are switched on before turning on your PC.

Is the application scanning the document using the correct settings?
Most scanner problems are related to the software controlling the scanner. Common problems include having the resolution (DPI) setting too high, causing massive files to be created.

Was the scanner switched on before the PC?
Many scanners, by the nature of their connection and the software that drives them, need to be switched on before the PC.

Has the scanner been unlocked since transportation?
Scanners have a locking feature for transportation. Check the scanner manual on how to lock and unlock your scanner during and after transportation.

Is there enough space on the hard disk for the image to be saved?
Scanners can produce very large image files. If you have insufficient hard disk or memory space to accommodate these files an error may be generated. Try reducing the number of colours and the resolution (DPI) of the scanner.

Common features of scanners

Is another application affecting the scanner software?

Scanners that use the parallel port can sometimes conflict with the software that controls the printer. The printer software is often represented as a small icon along the taskbar (bottom right). Try disabling this software first, then trying the scanner again.

1 **'Image Type'** allows you to set the number of colours to include in the scan. The higher the colour depth, the bigger the file. Hence, 'True color' creates a scan with over 16 million shades of colour. This is useful if you are scanning and reproducing a photographic image using a photographic printer. However, when scanning low-quality material or for output to the screen, lower colour depth produces much more manageable file sizes.

2 Many scanner drivers present a preview of the image to be scanned. You can normally fine-tune this by selecting an area within the preview scan and then selecting either **'Prescan'** or **'Scan'**.

3 The DPI (dots per inch) also affects the quality of the scan and the size of the file. As a rule of thumb, if you are scanning for on-screen uses such as creating images for a website, the DPI needs to be only around 75. If, however, you are scanning for a printed version, you should use a higher DPI, and one that is divisible by your printer's print resolution — e.g. if you have a 600 DPI printer, scanning at either 300 or 600 DPI will give you results as good as scanning at much higher resolutions, but without creating very big files.

FIXING GRAPHICS PROBLEMS

Most activities that PCs are used for require at least adequate graphics capability and, in the case of many games, fast, smooth and realistic graphics. Windows XP makes extensive use of graphics, compared with the first version of Windows, and without high-resolution graphics it would look anaemic. This section deals with some basic graphics troubleshooting.

COMMON PROBLEMS AND POSSIBLE CAUSES

Is the monitor plugged into the computer's VGA socket?
Check all the connections between the PC and the monitor. Check that no pins are bent in the plug at the end of the monitor's connection to the PC.

Is the colour depth suitable to the target application?
Many applications (especially video games) require a minimum number of colours to be displayed on the screen. If this colour depth is too low the application may look odd or not work. To get to Screen Properties, right-click on the Windows desktop and select **'Properties'**. See section 3.2.

Are the correct DirectX drivers installed?
DirectX is a standard created by Microsoft to help multimedia applications to work correctly. The DirectX software is updated by individual graphics card manufacturers to improve both performance and compatibility between software and their products. To test and update your DirectX and graphics card drivers follow the steps on the facing page.

Is the monitor switched on?
Check. If necessary, try another known working power lead.

Is the hardware acceleration affecting the graphics card performance?
The Display Properties screen also has advanced functions. From within these advanced functions you may be able to reduce the amount of hardware acceleration offered by a graphics card. This hardware acceleration can affect the reliability of the video device within older applications.

Is your monitor set to the correct screen resolution?
Many multimedia applications require a minimum screen resolution. This resolution is described as a horizontal and vertical value. Check the software's requirements and compare them to the settings in your Display Properties. Also check that you are using the correct refresh rate for your monitor (check documentation).

DirectX diagnostic

The DirectX diagnostic tool can be run by clicking on **'Start'**, then **'Run'**, typing in the **'Open'** box **'dxdiag'** and clicking **'OK'**.

Within this utility are several sections which can help diagnose DirectX software and facilities. The tab **'DirectX Files'** examines the DirectX files on your PC and reports on their likely reliability.

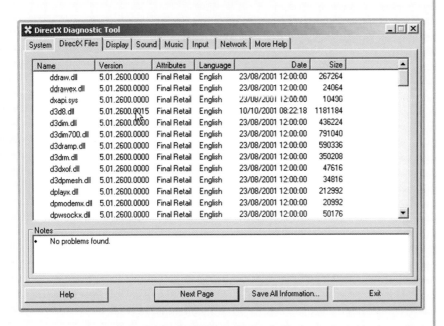

Re-installing graphics and DirectX software

STEP 1
Ascertain the make and model of your graphics card by clicking on the 'Display' tab in the DirectX diagnostic tool.

STEP 2
Ascertain which version of DirectX is installed on your PC from the 'System' tab as above.

STEP 3
Look at the website of your graphics card manufacturer for its latest drivers for your card. Follow the instructions to download and install the latest drivers if required.

STEP 4
Check that you have the latest DirectX software by going to Microsoft's DirectX website at www.microsoft.com/directx/ DirectX 8.1 is the latest version at the time of writing. It is supplied with Windows XP, but also works with Windows 98, ME and 2000, so download and install it if you have any of these versions of Windows. Users of Windows 95 should download DirectX 8.0a. See sections 4.13 and 4.14 for more on DirectX.

FIXING SOUND PROBLEMS

Sound has become very important in modern PCs. With the advent of DVD, Dolby surround-sound and the re-creation in the home of the cinema, it is possible to spend nearly £600 on top-of-the-range speakers and soundcard alone. This section looks at some of the basic problems to do with sound.

COMMON PROBLEMS AND POSSIBLE CAUSES

Are the speakers plugged into the correct speaker socket?
Check that the lead from the speakers to the PC is plugged into the correct socket. See section 1.9. On most PCs, the sockets are labelled. If not, trial and error will work and you will not damage your PC by choosing the wrong socket.

Is the hardware working correctly?
See section 1.10 for instructions on how to examine System Properties. See also the facing page.

Is the hardware acceleration affecting the soundcard performance?
The Volume Control utility may also have advanced functions. From within these advanced functions you may be able to reduce the amount of hardware acceleration offered by a soundcard. This hardware acceleration can affect the reliability of the sound device within older applications.

Are the speakers switched on?
Unlike hi-fi speakers, most computer versions have separate on/off buttons.

Is the volume muted in the sound control?
Right-click on the small speaker icon in the bottom right-hand corner and select '**Properties**'.
If the icon is not active you need to go into '**Control Panel**' and '**Sound**' and ensure '**place volume icon in the taskbar**' is ticked. See facing page.

Have the application's own volume controls been muted?
Many applications have their own volume controls, accessible through the menu system.

Is more than one program trying to use the soundcard?
Some software applications try to take full control of the soundcard while they are running. Even if these applications have been minimised they may interfere with the sound features of any program started subsequently.

System properties (sound)

In XP, select **'Start'**, **'Control Panel'** and **'System'**. You can then go to the **'Hardware'** tab and choose **'Device Manager'**.

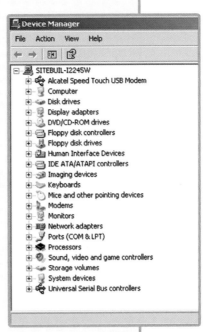

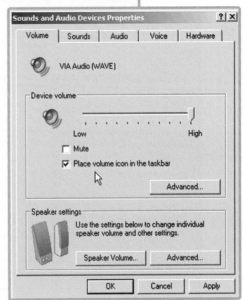

By right-clicking on the soundcard in Device Manager you may view the properties.

Within Control Panel, selecting **'Sounds and Audio Devices'** will show you if the speaker icon is active.

UPDATING WINDOWS

Microsoft makes available a variety of updates for all versions of Windows. These are of two sorts – critical and generally useful. Most of the critical ones either fix 'features' (otherwise known as bugs!) or block security holes. The latter is especially important if you use Internet Explorer as your browser and either Outlook or Outlook Express as your email client. The easiest way to access these updates is from the 'Tools' menu in Internet Explorer.

This will take you directly to the Windows Update site, from which you can access the updates for your version of Windows (where it exists) and Internet Explorer or Outlook.

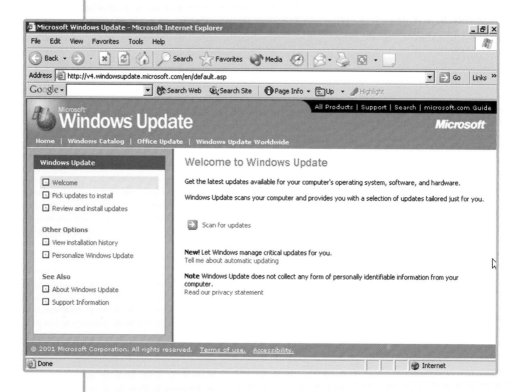

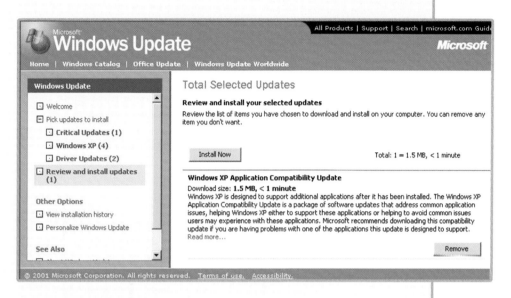

When you log on, Windows Update scans your PC to see what updates are available and give you a list of updates. This scan is carried out without sending any information to Microsoft.

Once you have chosen the updates you require (and the critical ones should be a priority), Windows Update takes you into the downloading and installing process.

After the update is finished you will usually be asked to restart Windows in order to complete the installation.

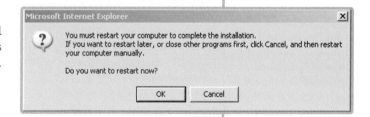

TROUBLESHOOTING WORD

A file by any other name

Although Microsoft Word is the most popular word-processing program, it has many versions and several rivals such as Lotus's SmartSuite, Corel's WordPerfect and Sun's Star Office (which is free). The current most commonly used versions of Microsoft Office are Office 97 and Office 2000. Office XP was released in May 2001. Earlier versions, such as Office 95, have had problems reading files created in later versions, and Microsoft released a patch to deal with that problem. One way of making all Office and other word-processing program files readable by every version is to save the files in RTF (rich text format). This can be especially helpful is you do not know the program the recipient of your document is using. To use the RTF format, simply use the **'Save As'** command from the File menu and choose the RTF format.

Microsoft Word is the most popular word-processing package in the world. Each version has offered improved features and more customisation over the previous one. But even though Word is quite a simple program, it has some quirks that can stump new users. This section answers some of the more common questions on Word.

I have spelt a word correctly, but the spell-checker insists that it is incorrect. What can I do?
The auto spell-checker in Windows often defaults to an American dictionary during installation. To change this to an English (UK) one, select from the menu bar: Tools/Options/Spelling and Grammar, then click on the **'Dictionaries'** button. You will be presented with a window where you can change the default language for the Word dictionary. Select English (UK) from the available options and then select OK.

Check the regional settings in Control Panel. They should be set for the UK.

You may have to restart Word for the changes to take effect.

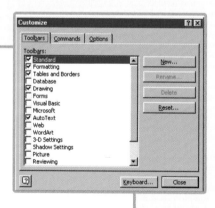

My Word area is overcrowded with toolbar icons. How can I remove the ones I don't use?
Toolbars are useful for placing commonly used commands within easy reach. However, as there are over 15 different toolbars, for tasks ranging from printing to drawing graphics, you may want to display only the ones you find useful. By clicking on View/Toolbars/Customise you can add or remove toolbars and even customise what commands appear on each toolbar.

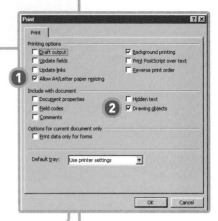

My documents look different when I print them out from how they look on screen. Why?

Print options (found under the File/Print menu, then the **'Option'** button) can fix this sort of problem. The most common is **1** the **'Allow A4/Letter paper resizing'** option. This option is used to reposition the text automatically if the paper in the printer does not match the page size. Turning this feature off will force Word to print to the paper without any transformation. **2** Make sure also that the **'Drawing objects'** option is ticked, otherwise any graphics will not be displayed.

I am partially sighted and have difficulty viewing the small icons on the toolbar. Is there anything I can do about this?

By using the zoom facility you can adjust your view of the text. However, to increase the size of the icons you need to select Tools/Customise/Options. If you tick **3** the **'Large icon'** button, all toolbar icons will double in size.

Where have my menus gone?

In Word (and Office) 2000 the menus can appear much shorter than in earlier versions.

The entries in this and other menus are not lost, they are just hidden. If you move your cursor over the **double-headed arrows,** they reappear. To overcome this 'feature' within Word, click on **'Tools'**, then **'Customize'**. In the **'Options'** tab, untick **'Menus show recently used commands first'**. This will restore all the menus, not only for Word, but also in the rest of the Office 2000 package (e.g. Excel and PowerPoint).

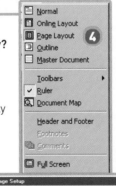

When I opened a document I was sent, it looked odd, and when I tried to print it out half the page was missing. Why?

The computer on which the document was originally created may have had different settings. Use the View command to cycle through the possible ways to look at your document. **4** **'Page Layout'** is the most commonly used mode because unlike the **'Normal'** mode it will also display graphics.

It is possible that the document was designed for an A3 printer. To check this, look under File/Page Setup. **5** From this window you may need to change your page orientation to landscape while changing your paper size back to A4. This will split an A3 (portrait) document into two A4 (landscape) documents, allowing your A4 printer to output it. However, you may need to tweak margin sizes as well to get the page to fit properly.

TROUBLESHOOTING FOR GAMES-PLAYERS (I)

Try before you buy

Before spending perhaps as much as £40 on a computer game, check out the reviews and buying advice in magazines, which also often give away demos of games on CDs. You can also try these using downloads from the Internet.

As far as Windows is concerned, games have had a chequered history. When the first version of Windows was released in 1985 all games were DOS-based, with fairly low-resolution, limited colour graphics. By the time Windows 98 was released, most games were high-resolution, multi-colour affairs. The majority worked well under Windows 98. As Windows ME is just a development of Windows 98, games that run well under Windows 98 generally work properly in Windows ME. However, once you shift to the other Windows family – represented by Windows NT, 2000 and XP – significant caveats have to be applied, although not so much to Windows XP.

Although Windows NT was aimed solely at the business sector where nobody is meant to play games, Windows 2000 has gained a foothold in the domestic market – especially for people who work from home and require a stable operating system. It became clear early on that Windows 2000 was unhappy with lots of popular games. This was for two main reasons. First, suppliers did not bother to release versions for Windows 2000. Second, because the operating system was specifically aimed at business users, Microsoft did not really work to develop a gaming platform. However, with Windows XP, all that has changed. As XP is designed to replace all earlier versions of Windows, facilitating the playing of games users either already own or are likely to buy is essential.

By and large, Windows XP does this well. With a few notable exceptions, including Microsoft's own popular 'Age of Empires', the vast majority of games will work under Windows XP. You may have to work at it a little, but all the advice you need to get games working is available from one of three sources: the games suppliers themselves, the Help facilities within XP, and the Internet.

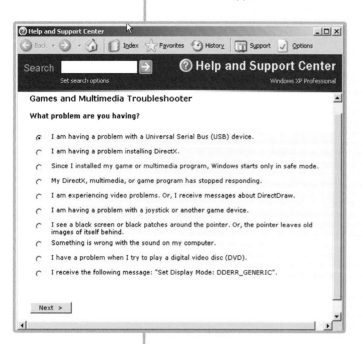

Computer games – from thoughtful strategy games to fast-paced action ones – sell in huge quantities these days. Their development has gone hand-in-hand with hardware development that allows vivid, smooth, fast and realistic 3D graphics so essential to modern games programs. Underpinning much of this gaming technology is a set of standards called Microsoft DirectX (and its components). Another key graphics language is OpenGL. Alongside these two key requirements (and you do not necessarily find an individual game using both) is a third – the graphics card in your PC and its drivers. If you have migrated to XP, properly working graphic-card drivers are vital.

The remainder of this section (and some of the next) focuses on DirectX and its diagnostic tools built into Windows.

The DirectX software that is supplied with Windows XP is version 8.1. If you are using Windows 98, 98SE, ME or Windows 2000, you can upgrade to DirectX 8.1 but anybody who uses Windows 95 can use only DirectX 8.0a. Always check with Microsoft's DirectX website: www.microsoft.com/directx

Use the Internet for advice

If you hope to use old games with XP carry out a search on the Internet (using a search engine like Google) on the topic 'Games under XP'. This will give you several useful links to sites that list known issues with hundreds of games or other applications running in XP.

4 | Basic troubleshooting

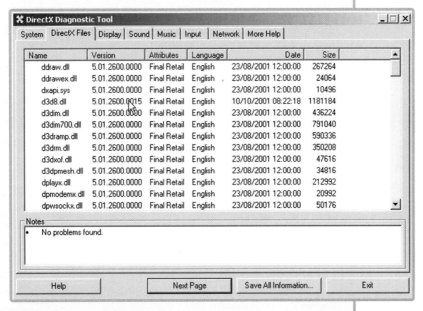

The first page of information describes what DirectX believes your system has by way of resources.

TROUBLESHOOTING FOR GAMES-PLAYERS (II)

4 | Basic troubleshooting

Know your rights

PC games manufacturers cannot test their games with every possible combination of hardware and software. If you buy a game and, despite troubleshooting, it still does not work, you can return it for a refund or credit. Even if the shop tests the game on its computer system and it works, its system will not be identical to yours so this will not be an excuse for the shop to dismiss your claim.

The spread (albeit slowly) of broadband Internet access is of great interest to the serious games player. Online gaming with multiple users simultaneously playing complex games around the world is a growing activity. However, for many home users with slow, dial-up connections, games are more likely to be running just on their PCs.

For both sets of users, DirectX is a key component. This section gives some more information about DirectX diagnostics.

The two main information panels under the 'Sound' tab give details of the name of the soundcard, the driver version and whether they have been signed (authorised) by Microsoft.

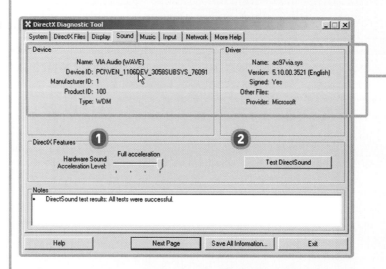

1 Modern soundcards have a form of acceleration that relieves some of the work of your processor and instead allows the soundcard to process information itself. This acceleration can help performance but may cause errors. You can reduce the amount of acceleration with this lever to reduce errors caused by this feature.

2 You can test the various playback qualities and sampling rates using the test DirectSound button. The test will use different features of your soundcard. If some of these settings fail to play make sure you use settings which do work for your games.

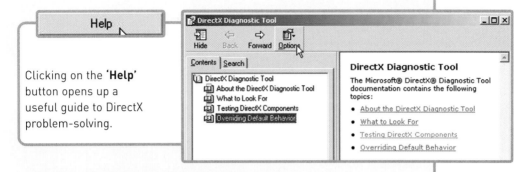

Clicking on the **'Help'** button opens up a useful guide to DirectX problem-solving.

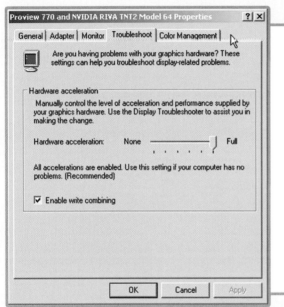

Right-clicking on the desktop and selecting **'Properties'** allows you to change some of the settings of your graphics card. Reducing hardware acceleration may solve problems you have playing games, but can also reduce performance. You may need to experiment to find the right balance.

The need for speed and power

Games have driven (and still drive) many advances in computer graphics. For the games enthusiast a fast, powerful graphics card is essential. Prices for a card with 32Mb RAM upwards range from £25 to over £300. Shop around and read computer magazines to get an idea of what you want. Graphics cards are a frequent topic of detailed reviews. Because the choice may seem overwhelming, set an affordable budget and stick to it.

Internet gaming

Playing games online with people around the world is a fast-growing activity. There are a number of websites devoted to this activity, one of them being http://internetgames.about.com/mbody.htm

Multi-user games are not new: they started in the 1980s with multi-user dungeon MUD games which were, in the first instance, purely text games of strategy. Another hugely popular activity in this field is chess. One of the best sites for this is www.chessclub.com/, which can have thousands of players online at any one time. Some games-playing software is free and a useful site for this is www.freeloader.com/en/

This section deals with solving more serious PC problems. These problems generally occur when a piece of hardware or software has failed or is producing errors. Before you start getting out screwdrivers and anti-static wrist straps, it is worth checking all the paperwork that came with the system. The standard warranty for a new PC is one year. Some companies offer two years and many will offer an extension to three years for a fee payable at the time of purchase. Given that you have already paid for this service as part of the PC's purchase price, getting a properly trained engineer to fix your PC for free is always the best solution.

A word of warning, however: most companies do not consider software problems (even if the software came with the computer) to be their responsibility and may require additional payment to solve these types of problems. Your supplier may offer a technical support telephone line at premium rates. Charges of up to £1 per minute are not unknown, so beware before phoning. If your problem does not stop you emailing, look for a support email address. This can be as effective and has the virtue of both being cheap and avoiding telephone queues.

For older, or second-hand, machines, enforcing a warranty agreement may not be possible. Unless you have a very obscure make of PC, almost any of the 5,000+ PC repair specialists in the UK should be able to fix your PC but the labour cost will be quite high. For example, the labour cost of replacing a broken floppy-disk drive – which can be purchased for about £10 – may exceed £40. Hence, this section covers simple fixes which could save you some painful repair bills.

Thankfully, most errors are caused by software problems and as such can be fixed without the use of screwdrivers or new components. The skill lies in understanding the way a machine works and making educated guesses at what the problem might be. No book could cover every possible problem faced by a PC owner and every possible solution. A good tip, however, is to remember, if you are about to change a setting, to note down what it was before you changed it. If the troubleshooting does not work, you can always change it back. Remember, Windows XP provides the highly useful **'System Restore'** facility. This can be a sanity restorer if you make a software or hardware change that does not work.

ADVANCED TROUBLESHOOTING

5.1 **PC architecture**
A fuller description of the PC system

5.2 **The BIOS**
The Basic Input Output System

5.3 **PC boot-up examined**
What happens when you first turn on a PC and
how this can help with troubleshooting

5.4 **Bootlog**
A useful tool for the troubleshooter

5.5 **Safe mode**
How this special diagnostic mode works

5.6 **Solving software conflicts**
Tips for solving more complex software problems

5.7 **Solving hardware conflicts**
Tips for solving more complex hardware problems

5.8 **Re-installing Windows**
If a Windows problem cannot be fixed,
re-installing Windows is a drastic, but effective, measure

5 | Advanced troubleshooting

PC ARCHITECTURE

For advanced troubleshooting on a PC it helps to have some understanding of the fundamentals of a PC's bits and pieces. As in a car's engine, it is all the parts working together that makes the machine run smoothly. Often, when one part seems to be faulty, the problem actually lies elsewhere. With PCs, one of the most common problems arises when you try to print. The fault may be with the software that drives the printer rather than with the actual printer. This section aims to give you an insight into PC fundamentals.

The diagram opposite shows the elements of a PC.

Starting up the PC

As the PC is turned on, power goes to each hardware device (**keyboard**, **storage mediums**, **RAM** and **processor**) and each in turn is tested by the **BIOS & chipset** on the motherboard.

As each **hardware** device responds, **RAM** (Random Access Memory) is loaded with its settings and a small program to start up **Windows**.

As **Windows** starts it takes the device settings from **RAM** and loads them into the drivers, which make further checks before starting up the **system applications** which may rely on these drivers. Once these **system applications** are started, **Windows** is ready to execute **software applications**.

Using software

When you use a software application, the PC follows a set pattern of activities to accomplish the task. For example, if you are word processing, as you press the A key on the **keyboard**, a signal is sent via the **chipset** to the **resource manager**, which in turn passes on the request to the driver which monitors the **keyboard** for Windows.

This keystroke is passed to the word-processing **application**, which then sends the command for processing to the **processor**, where the application program calculates what to do with the key press.

In our example the word-processing software decides to create the letter A in the chosen position in the document. Another chain of events is started to display this new character. This sequence finally sends the letter A to the **output device**, in this case the **screen**.

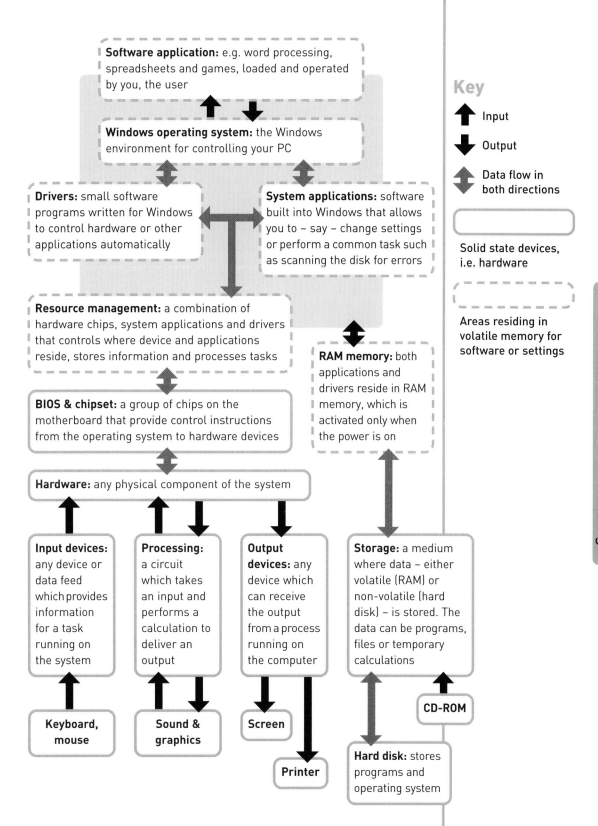

Software application: e.g. word processing, spreadsheets and games, loaded and operated by you, the user

Windows operating system: the Windows environment for controlling your PC

Drivers: small software programs written for Windows to control hardware or other applications automatically

System applications: software built into Windows that allows you to – say – change settings or perform a common task such as scanning the disk for errors

Resource management: a combination of hardware chips, system applications and drivers that controls where device and applications reside, stores information and processes tasks

RAM memory: both applications and drivers reside in RAM memory, which is activated only when the power is on

BIOS & chipset: a group of chips on the motherboard that provide control instructions from the operating system to hardware devices

Hardware: any physical component of the system

Input devices: any device or data feed which provides information for a task running on the system

Processing: a circuit which takes an input and performs a calculation to deliver an output

Output devices: any device which can receive the output from a process running on the computer

Storage: a medium where data – either volatile (RAM) or non-volatile (hard disk) – is stored. The data can be programs, files or temporary calculations

Keyboard, mouse

Sound & graphics

Screen

Printer

CD-ROM

Hard disk: stores programs and operating system

Key

Input

Output

Data flow in both directions

Solid state devices, i.e. hardware

Areas residing in volatile memory for software or settings

5 | Advanced troubleshooting

THE BIOS

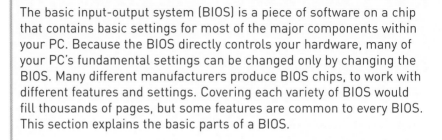

The basic input-output system (BIOS) is a piece of software on a chip that contains basic settings for most of the major components within your PC. Because the BIOS directly controls your hardware, many of your PC's fundamental settings can be changed only by changing the BIOS. Many different manufacturers produce BIOS chips, to work with different features and settings. Covering each variety of BIOS would fill thousands of pages, but some features are common to every BIOS. This section explains the basic parts of a BIOS.

Warning!

Many Windows utilities contained within the Control Panel are used by other programs. Removing key applications such as 'Dial up networking' may affect Internet and facsimile settings.

The basic input-output system (BIOS)

The first screen of text you see whenever you start up your PC tells you what processor, or CPU (central processing unit), you have and how much RAM is fitted to your PC. This screen may appear fleetingly; pressing down the Pause key should slow it down so you can inspect it closely. The screen also refers to the BIOS. If you press the key that is mentioned at the bottom of the screen – normally Delete, F1 or F2 — you get into the Setup utility, which lets you alter the **BIOS settings**. The BIOS, a special chip (sometimes removable) burned on to the motherboard, contains software and information about your PC and how to start it up. Its components include the boot-loader, which copies enough information into RAM to allow the PC to start up, and the Power-On Self-Test (POST), which checks that the memory, graphics cards and other elements are working properly.

Main screen

When you arrive at the main screen of the BIOS you will see basic system information, e.g. speed and type of processor and amount of RAM fitted. These are automatically detected and you cannot change the settings but it is a useful check when upgrading RAM or processors. However, you should take a note of the BIOS version. It may be possible to download an update (check the version number against the manufacturer's website first). The update may enable you to use new features for devices that have been produced since the PC was manufactured.

Basic BIOS options

Before you take a look at your BIOS, you should note that this book provides only broad guidelines. BIOS manufacturers may develop different BIOS for different motherboards, even customising a BIOS for an individual PC manufacturer. But despite the differences of detail, the general principles behind them remain the same. You need to save the changes for any alterations to take effect.

Drives

You can access some quite advanced options even from the main screen. Your hard disk is probably set to Auto type, and it is best to leave it this way. However, if you set type to User and turn off Logical Block Addressing (a factory preset) you can change some of the size settings. This should be done with extreme caution but might let you squeeze some extra capacity out of an old hard disk.

Time and date

You can change your PC's time and date using this option. The date may appear in American format (mm/dd/yyyy). It is easy to change the time and date in Windows Control Panel.

Boot order

On this Boot screen, you can change the order in which your PC looks for a disk containing system files, which it must find in order to start up. Normally, it will check your floppy drive, then hard disk, then CD-ROM. You can change this order: if you move the floppy drive further down, it will stop anyone starting your machine from a floppy disk (i.e. without having to give a password, thereby bypassing any software security settings).

Ports

Under **'Peripheral Configuration'** (usually on the **'Advanced'** screen) you can change settings for your serial and parallel ports. Memory and Interrupt settings need be changed only to avoid conflicts. A conflict occurs when two devices are trying to use the same IRQ (see Glossary). You can also check the parallel port mode. It should be at least bi-directional, but EPP and ECP are enhanced modes that offer faster data transfer for devices like printers and scanners.

Power management

If you have a separate Power screen, you can control your system's power-saving behaviour. If you enable Power Management Support, your PC will switch off automatically when you tell it to. You can also control whether devices like the system fan, hard disk and screen **'go to sleep'** after a period of inactivity, and how long this should be.

Wake on LAN/modem ring

Some motherboards have a BIOS which supports this feature, which allows your PC to be switched on automatically by certain events such as activity on the local area network (LAN) or, for home users, the arrival of a fax. WOL, as it is called, normally works with a network card or a modem.

Password (security)

You may have a separate Security screen, or this option may appear on the main screen. It is possible to set a user password to control access to your PC, and a supervisor password to control access to these BIOS screens. You need to type each twice: don't forget these passwords, as without your BIOS password you will not able to start the system or change BIOS settings.

Cache

You can turn memory cache on or off from the Advanced screen. This is a super-fast type of memory which speeds up your PC by storing frequently used instructions for quick access. **'Cache ECC support'** is an option you can select for error correction: turning it on slows your PC very slightly but checks the cache for errors and improves reliability.

Event logging

Event logging can keep a check on any problems faced by your system as it boots up. Many of these sound worse than they really are – e.g. a stuck key can produce a **'dead keyboard error'** – but it can be interesting to keep an eye on them. If the event log produces an increasing number of problems, you may have an intermittent hardware fault with memory or your hard disk.

Advanced BIOS features

If you go to the Advanced screen and choose **'Resource Configuration'** you can change settings which nowadays it is better to alter through Windows System Properties. However, if old expansion cards cause trouble, it may be useful to allocate them specific areas of memory or particular IRQs here (see Glossary for more on IRQs). Do this only in conjunction with the card's documentation.

PC BOOT-UP EXAMINED

When a PC is turned on, the system performs many tasks before the Windows operating system starts. This process is called booting. When Windows fails to start correctly or reports errors constantly, these problems can be fixed by altering the boot-up process. This section explains how a boot-up works and how to correct problems that may occur during the boot-up phase.

BIOS tests hardware:
memory, floppy disk, keyboard, hard disk

If a fault occurs during the BIOS test, the BIOS generates an error message and may beep. This message may indicate hardware problems, such as a loose connection, failed component or incorrect settings in the BIOS.

Autoexec.bat runs, **Config.sys** runs (only 98)
The Autoexec.bat and Config.sys files load DOS programs into the memory before Windows loads. These are typically anti-virus programs or security software. Removing these applications (which may be corrupt or causing errors) can help a successful boot.

Applications in Startup group run
The Startup group loads applications which have been set to run automatically. If these applications are causing errors, Windows may fail to start.

Boot problems
In Windows XP there is a feature called the **Recovery Console**. This very useful utility can help you in a variety of situations in which your PC does not start or will start correctly. But – and this is a big 'but' – you must install Recovery Console before you use the PC: that means as soon as you take your new Windows XP PC out of the box.

Boot sector
The boot sector is a special part of the disk that contains instructions for loading the operating system into the computer's memory. It can become corrupted, especially by a boot-sector virus. If you have installed anti-virus software, the recovery/rescue disk created by you during installation becomes vital.

Windows checks to see if hardware has changed and is working. If hardware is o.k., it loads hardware drivers. Next it loads system applications, such as Start bar, desktop and fonts.

As Windows boots, it makes a rudimentary check on all the hardware and software it believes are installed. If these checks are passed, Windows continues. If not, it automatically tries to fix any problems. If the problems are unfixable, Windows may crash during this phase. Using the safe mode (see section 5.5) can help with troubleshooting.

Fixing a corrupted boot sector

The boot sector is the most important part of the hard disk because without it the computer cannot start up correctly. The boot sector, like any part of a computer hard disk, is susceptible to data corruption through wear and tear.

If your PC fails to boot and shows messages like **'Unable to load command.com'** or **'Drive not ready'** try these simple troubleshooting steps:

- make sure no floppy disk is in the drive and restart your PC
- examine the BIOS to make sure that the primary hard-disk drive is still listed
- try booting into safe mode (see section 5.5).

One situation in which a PC fails to boot properly occurs in older PCs where the little battery that stores key PC settings runs out. All motherboards have these batteries. In PCs built since 1997 it is a round, 3v lithium cell battery.

A common sign of this problem is a line on the start-up screen that says **'Press F1 to continue'** or similar. If your PC was bought after 2000, this is unlikely to happen. With some PCs a dead memory battery can actually make the PC seem totally dead.

If safe mode and other start-up options do not work, you can consider using the Recovery Console.

This method is recommended only if you are an advanced user who can use basic commands to identify and locate problem drivers and files. In addition, you must be an **'administrator'** and not a **'limited user'** to use the Recovery Console.

Using the Recovery Console, you can enable and disable services, format drives, read and write data on a local drive, and perform many other administrative tasks. The Recovery Console is particularly useful if you need to repair your system by copying a file from a floppy disk or CD-ROM to your hard drive, or if you need to reconfigure a service that is preventing your computer from starting properly.
There are two ways to start the Recovery Console.

- If you are unable to start your computer, you can run the Recovery Console from your setup CD.
- As an alternative, you can install the Recovery Console on your computer to make it available in case you are unable to restart Windows. You can then select the Recovery Console option from the list of available operating systems on start-up.

After you start the Recovery Console you will have to choose which installation you want to log on to (if you have a dual-boot or multiple-boot system) and you will have to log on with your administrator password.

The console provides commands you can use to do simple operations such as changing to a different directory or viewing a directory, and more powerful operations such as fixing the boot sector. You can access Help for the commands in the Recovery Console by typing **'help'** at the Recovery Console command prompt.

Bearing in mind that a PC that will not boot is rather 'sick' and you have a potentially serious problem, it is worth exploring the Recovery Console information from the Help section in the Start menu on your PC.

BOOTLOG

During the XP boot-up process, Windows can create a useful file called **'ntbtlog.txt'** that is stored on the hard disk after boot-up in the Windows directory. This file provides information about which hardware devices and software drivers have installed. With this data you can take action to fix problems. This section explains how to examine ntbtlog.txt for indications of problems.

Creating the file

To create this file you need to boot into safe mode (see section 5.5) and choose **'Enable Boot Logging'**.

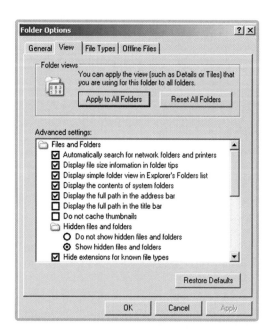

To view the ntbtlog.txt file, which is normally hidden, you first need to make visible all hidden files. Double-click on **'My Computer'** and then double-click on the **'C:'** drive. On the main menu of this drive, select **'View'**, **'Folder Options'**, **'View'**, then make sure that the **'Show all files'** button is selected under the hidden files attribute.

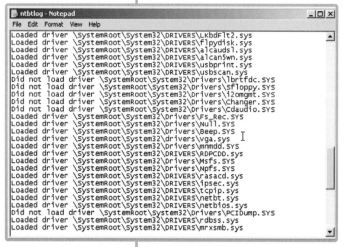

If you now look back in the main C: drive you will see some additional files. If you double-click on the file called **'ntbtlog.txt'** it will load this file into the basic Windows word processor (WordPad). This file can have thousands of lines of information, describing what happened during the last Windows boot-up, including whether each hardware and Windows device installed correctly.

If the device loaded correctly, the word **'success'** will appear next to the device. The words **'not loaded'** can also appear. If you see **'failed'** next to a driver name, you need to find out to what it refers.

By using WordPad's built-in search utility, you can search bootlog for instances when a device failed. To use this feature press Ctrl + F, then type **'Fail'** as the search string. Each time you press the F3 key it will search for another failed device.

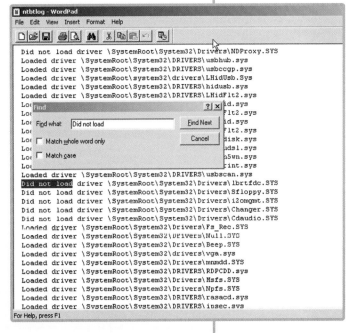

To find out more about the file which has not loaded or has failed to load you need to locate it and examine its properties. To locate the file, use the Search facility from the Start menu. Once located, right-click on the file name to examine its properties.

If you follow the steps described above for each failed file, you can find out what has failed and what hardware or software it relates to. This is a process of deduction. Common sense is also useful. If you are having problems with a new soundcard, for instance, it may be as well to check the manufacturer's website to see if there is a new or more recent driver. The above process may help you identify the date and version number of your existing driver.

SAFE MODE

Windows safe mode is a special way of starting the Windows operating system when errors prevent it starting in the normal way. When in safe mode, many of Windows' more advanced functions are disabled, which allows you to perform permanent fixes to errant applications and Windows features. This section covers how to get to the Windows safe mode and how to use it to fix problems. Note that safe mode is the only way in which you can access your files should Windows product activation (see section 2.10) disable access to your PC.

```
Windows Advanced Options Menu
Please select an option

Safe Mode
Safe Mode with Networking
Safe Mode with Command Prompt

Enable Boot Logging
Enable VGA Mode
Last Known Good Configuration (your most recent settings that worked)
Directory Service Restore Mode (Windows domain controller only)
Debugging mode

Start Windows Normally
Reboot
Return to OS Choices Menu

Use the up and down arrow keys to move the highlight to your choice
```

Entering safe mode

To enter safe mode, press the F8 key as your PC boots up. At this point you are presented with a menu. Here, select **'Safe mode'** and Windows will begin.

Differences in versions of Windows

Safe mode is a feature in all versions of Windows. You access it in the same way in each version by pressing F8 as the PC boots. The menu you see in Windows XP is more extensive than the one in earlier versions, but the most commonly used options are the same.

Safe mode starts using only basic files and drivers (mouse, except serial mice; monitor; keyboard; mass storage; base video; default system devices; and no network connections). If your computer does not start successfully using safe mode, you might need to use the Recovery Console feature to repair your system.

Safe mode helps you diagnose problems. If a symptom does not reappear when you start in safe mode, you can eliminate the default settings and minimum device drivers as possible causes. If a newly added device or a changed driver is causing problems, you can use safe mode to remove the device or reverse the change.

There are circumstances in which safe mode will not be able to help you, such as when Windows system files that are required to start the system are corrupted or damaged. In this case, the Recovery Console may help you.

Limitations of safe mode

Safe mode has its limitations:
• you cannot install applications in safe mode
• some applications may not work in safe mode
• many devices will not work in safe mode.

Safe mode is a good way to get files off your system in an emergency, if Windows will not start correctly. However, note that files can be written only to a floppy disk or another hard drive already in the system.

Common problems that can be fixed in safe mode:

• if you have set a screen resolution which garbles your screen, safe mode resets your screen drivers back to a known good setting. From here you can select a resolution which is suitable and then restart your machine
• if you have installed a program in the start-up group which is now stopping Windows from starting, safe mode ignores this group and allows you to remove this program
• if your hardware has been upgraded and is now stopping Windows from starting, safe mode loads minimal driver support and allows device drivers to be removed
• if an application crashes when the uninstall routine is started, you can uninstall it in safe mode.

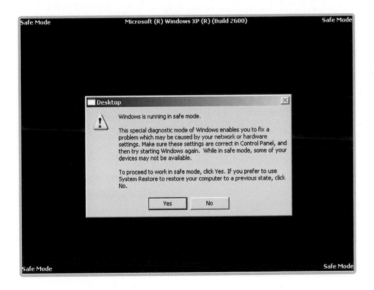

ScanDisk and Defrag

In Windows 95 and Windows 98, it is always a good idea to boot into safe mode before running ScanDisk or disk defragmenter. This is especially true if you normally use an anti-virus package. Windows 95 is particularly prone to constantly restart Defrag if an anti-virus package is running. Safe mode does not load the anti-virus package, thus allowing Defrag to run without interruption.

SOLVING SOFTWARE CONFLICTS

Solving more complex problems involving software can sometimes be a real challenge. Windows XP is the best version of Windows for dealing with conflicts that can occur, especially those created by trying to use old programs – sometimes called 'legacy' programs. This section suggests some ways for dealing with these problems. Although it focuses on Windows XP, it also offers tips for those using Windows ME.

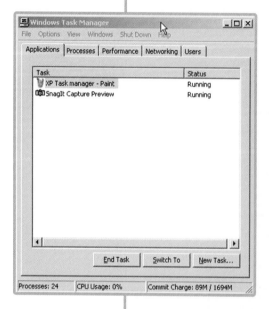

Even when Windows first loads and before you might think you have loaded a program, several programs may already be running in the background. These may be performing essential Windows tasks or functions at the request of the user. Common background tasks include anti-virus software, graphics-card utilities, printer drivers and media players. When, say, you are working with Word, unknown to you several other programs and utilities, such as anti-virus software, Internet browser and email, may be running at the same time.

Sometimes an application stops working or crashes the moment it is started. One common cause is a conflict with another program. One method of identifying problems is a process of elimination. You can shut down an errant program in XP by using Task Manager. This is loaded by pressing Ctrl + Alt + Del simultaneously. Select the task and then click on **'End Task'**. Before you start shutting down a running task, check which other tasks are running.

By using the System Information tool (see sections 4.3 and 4.4) and by looking under the 'Software Environment' attribute, you can find out which applications are currently running on your system. Here you could choose which applications to suspend in order to try solving a conflict. As a rule of thumb, anything listed as part of Windows should be left alone.

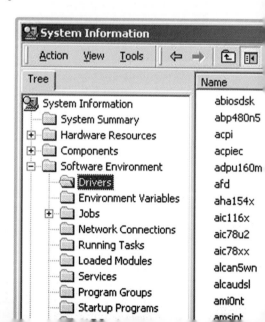

Some strategies for solving Windows problems

- Fax software (often supplied with modems) can conflict with Internet connections: shut it down.
- Anti-virus software can cause conflicts. Try closing it down temporarily.
- Games hardware (joysticks) control software can cause conflict with devices such as keyboards.
- If the driver software for a device is old, it may not work with newer applications or versions of Windows. Check the manufacturer's website for a compatible driver. This is especially true for Windows ME and XP.
- Some tasks require another application to be loaded before they will work.
- Check the Windows Update site for latest drivers. See www.windowsupdate.microsoft.com
- Try and think ahead by anticipating problems. Go to http://support.microsoft.com/directory
- Use the Internet to find answers. Go to www.google.com (or another search engine) and type in a question. You will be surprised at what turns up.
- Use Dr Watson, a diagnostic tool. Go to **'Start'** and **'Run'**, and in Windows ME or earlier type **'drwatson'** and press **'Enter'**. In Windows XP type **'drwtsn32'**. Dr Watson may put your mind at ease about error messages (some of which are singularly unhelpful and even misleading). Once launched, the program will sit around and leap into action at the first hint of errors. It gathers details about what has just happened and writes them to a log file. Go here – http://support.microsoft.com/ – and search through the TechNet link for the Knowledge Base article Q275481 'How to troubleshoot program faults with Dr Watson'.
- Learn how to use System Restore in Windows ME and XP.
- Read the Windows Help files. They are especially useful in XP.

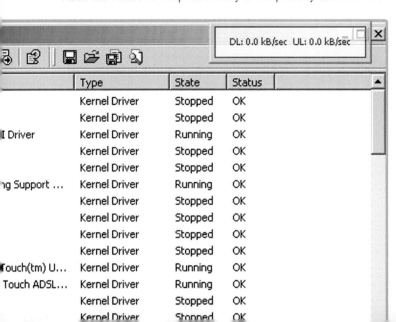

SOLVING HARDWARE CONFLICTS

Windows warnings in Device Manager

 This symbol may appear next to a device: it means that Windows believes that the driver is not working correctly. Unless you notice a problem, this can indicate that the driver is not entirely compatible but the device is still working.

 A red cross through a device indicates that it has either been disabled by the user or has not been configured properly. Some devices, such as external scanners or digital cameras, may display this symbol if turned off, when the PC is first booted up.

 A yellow question mark denotes a device that Windows does not recognise. This is not always an error as some devices talk directly to the hardware, circumventing Windows.

If you buy a new PC it is unlikely to come with any hardware or software conflicts as the supplier should ensure that the machine is in perfect working order. Problems may occur when you add new hardware or programs. The section aims to offer some help in dealing with such difficulties.

One of the innovations introduced with Windows 95 was the concept of **'Plug and play'**. This aimed to make the installation of new devices (soundcards, graphics cards, modems, etc.) seamless as Windows sorted out the resources needed by the new device. As with all new ideas, getting it to work properly was a little more difficult. One of the first hurdles resulted from the fact that not all existing devices were plug and play. Later versions of Windows (with the notable exception of Windows NT) have tackled this challenge with increasing success. Windows XP works very well with plug and play devices and handles older hardware competently. Without doubt, the work of the manufacturers of devices has been crucial in turning plug and play into a reliable concept.

Conflicts might occur when two devices wish to use the same resources. Dealing with that is fairly straightforward.

In all versions of Windows you have the facility to identify, remove and re-install a device or update a driver by using the Control Panel. There are variations between versions of Windows, but in all cases you access Control Panel from the Start menu. After choosing **'Control Panel'**, double-click on

the **'System'** icon. In XP you must then choose **'Hardware'** and **'Device Manager'**. This will reveal the window shown above. With Windows 95, 98 and ME simply double-click as above, but only select the **'Device Manager'** tab. Select the device you wish to modify (remove, say) and click on the appropriate button (**'Remove'**, in the example). Again, there are minor differences between versions of Windows. In XP you have to select a device and then choose the **'Update Driver'** or **'Disable'** or **'Uninstall'** icon at the top of the Device Manager window. It is much the same in Windows 2000.

If re-installing the device does not work, you may have to change the driver's settings or change the driver for a newer version.

Each device has a general information screen, containing manufacturer and version details.

Some devices have additional information and configuration tabs.

In this case, the Status tab is available. Once it is selected, more detailed information about the device becomes available. This is useful for cataloguing your system and for deciding whether you need to upgrade a device driver.

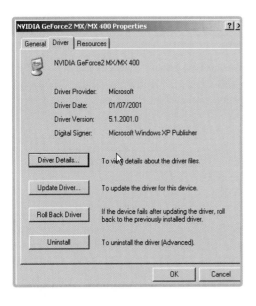

All versions of Windows allow you to check a device's driver details through Control Panel. A useful alternative is to use the Help feature found on the Start menu in all versions. Windows XP is especially good in the way it provides information about your devices through the **'Tools'** option within the **'Help and Support Center'** accessed through the Start menu.

RE-INSTALLING WINDOWS

If you have a major problem with Windows which seems impossible to solve you may feel that the only solution is to re-install Windows. This is an extreme step to take – although, on occasions, it may really be the best thing to do. This section looks at the implications, the requirements and the methods.

Re-installing Windows can mean one of two things: re-installing Windows over an existing version, or erasing everything on your system and starting completely from scratch (i.e., reloading Windows, all your software applications and the device drivers). You will need to **back up all your important documents and data**.

Note that you must not re-install XP without contacting Microsoft by telephone because of the Windows product activation feature (see section 2.10).

Does the version of Windows matter?

In a word – yes. The procedures for re-installing Windows 95, 98 and ME are broadly similar. For Windows 2000 and XP they are very different. Windows XP has clever facilities within it that may well mean you never have to re-install. The procedures for re-installing Windows over your existing version are outlined below. The later versions of Windows (2000 and XP) do not have the start-up disk of the earlier versions. Both are designed to be installed from a bootable CD and to have very different file systems from the earlier versions.

1 The easiest way to re-install Windows 98 or ME is to place the original Windows CD-ROM in the drive and the Windows start-up disk in the floppy drive and restart your system. The machine will now boot and prompt you to start the installation procedure. For 2000 and XP, boot from the CD.

2 Another method is to start the Windows setup procedure from within Windows by using the **'Find'** command to locate the Setup.exe file – often located in C:\windows\options\cabs – and then double-click on it.

3 The third method is to start the PC and, when the words **'Starting Windows'** appear, press the F8 key. This will bring up a special menu from which you need to select the **'Safe mode command prompt'**.

If you have re-installed Windows over an existing version and the system still exhibits problems, you can re-install Windows from scratch. This requires some planning. You will need your original Windows installation CD and the unique installation code that came with the pack. Any applications, such as word processing, which came with your PC should also be available on CD-ROM. Your PC manufacturer has a legal requirement to supply these.

For Windows 95, 98 and ME a start-up disk is also required and should have been created when you first received your PC. If you have not created one of those and you can still run Windows 95, 98 or ME – despite your problems – now is the time to create one. Get yourself a blank, formatted floppy and go to **'Start'**, **'Control Panel'** and double-click on **'Add, Remove Programs'**. Select the third tab and create your start-up disk. If you have upgraded to Windows XP and have kept your Windows 98 start-up disk, it can still be used to carry out a clean installation of XP.

Now carry out the following steps for a clean installation of Windows 98.

1. Place the start-up disk in your PC and restart the system. (See section 5.2 and make sure your PC boots from the floppy drive.)
2. If asked, boot with CD-ROM support.
3. At the A:\ prompt type **Deltree C:\windows/s**. This will delete all of the Windows directories (and could take some minutes).
4. Place the Windows CD-ROM in the drive and follow the instructions supplied with the CD.
5. Re-install your main software applications.

Re-installing Windows 2000 and XP

Having to re-install Windows 2000 or XP is a very unusual occurrence, as these two versions of Windows rarely fail to work properly.

However, with both Windows 2000 and XP you should create an emergency repair disk. This is done from the Backup option accessed from **'Start'**, **'Programs'**, **'Accessories'** and **'System Tools'**. In Windows XP you have a choice of running the Backup Wizard or choosing **'Advanced Mode'**. If you choose the latter, you can go straight to the **'Automated System Recovery'** Wizard, where you can create the ASR disk.

Both Windows 2000 and XP contain detailed information about the process of recovering and repairing Windows if you click on **'Start'** and **'Help'**.

One reason why the PC is such a powerful machine is that it has potential for being upgraded. Most upgrades can be carried out by the user, but the huge variety of different PC designs and configurations can sometimes make even the simplest upgrade tricky.

All new hardware comes with the manufacturer's installation instructions and details of the system requirements for the new piece of kit. These specifications focus on the amount of RAM, type of operating system, the make and model of the processor and what other components are within the computer. The manufacturer will also indicate what free slots within the chassis or on the motherboard the new device will need before it can be installed successfully.

Before you upgrade or install any new devices, check whether your PC matches the required specification. Most of this can be gleaned from the system information screens (see chapter 1) but sometimes the only way to find out if your PC has the required bays or slots is to look inside the case. If the specification is o.k., read this chapter's generic instructions for upgrading the part in question, but be aware that they may not be suitable for all types of product, and **always follow the manufacturer's instructions**.

Many upgrades, especially those involving external USB, parallel or SCSI devices, are very simple, needing only the correct software to carry them out. For other upgrades you need to plug a new card into the computer's motherboard and then run the software. Upgrading a motherboard or a processor is more difficult and could damage both the new parts and the PC if done incorrectly. These types of upgrades are not for the novice. Experienced users do carry out such tasks, but if you are even a little doubtful, leave it to a professional. It could save you a lot of money.

The dangers of working inside the PC
The PC is an electrical device. If you try to open it while it is still switched on, you risk a fatal shock. Also, the static electric charge we all carry in our bodies can ruin the sensitive electronic components within the computer and/or its peripherals.

UPGRADING AND REPLACING HARDWARE

TOOLS OF THE TRADE

Most PCs are made to be easily serviceable. Simple cross-head (Phillips) and flat-head screwdrivers are all you will need in most cases.

Some PC manufacturers use special security screws to prevent tampering or to secure components with no serviceable parts such as power supplies or the insides of hard disks.

To protect yourself and your PC

- Always switch the PC off, and then turn it off at the wall, but leave it plugged in – this will ensure that the PC chassis remains earthed.

- Before touching any components, always touch a metal part of the PC chassis to discharge any static harmlessly. Ideally, buy an anti-static wristband and connect this to the PC whenever you are working on it to ensure that you remain earthed and cannot build up a static charge.

- Never open up the power supply. Because it is a transformer, even when it is switched off it can carry high residual voltages. If it is faulty, replace the entire unit: there are no user-serviceable parts inside (the same applies to monitors).

- Do not open up your screen: doing this could mean a deadly shock.

- When working with chips, try not to touch any of the pins or connectors: these carry any static shock right to the heart of the chip, burning out transistors.

6 | Upgrading and replacing hardware

UPGRADING RAM

Where to buy RAM

Many large computer centres offer free fitting for memory purchased from them or charge a flat rate for fitting upgrades. This can add a significant amount to the cost of a RAM upgrade, which is always cheaper bought online or via mail order. If you are careful, the task is straightforward.

Warning!

Memory is very sensitive to static electricity, so you should always take anti-static precautions before you remove or replace memory modules (see also page 131).

- **Ensure the PC is still plugged in to the mains power but the wall socket is turned off.**

- **Touch the fingers of both hands on a metal part of the PC chassis to remove static electricity from your body before handling any memory modules.**

Random access memory (RAM) is essential for the operation of your PC. Adding more RAM to your system – a relatively simple upgrade – can improve the performance of every aspect of your machine. This section covers how to identify the type of memory you need to buy and how to fit it into your system safely.

Knowing what memory to buy

Most new PCs tend to be sold with 64Mb or 128Mb of RAM pre-installed. For simple tasks such as word processing, Internet access and home finance, this is generally sufficient. If multiple applications are running and Windows needs more RAM, it uses the hard disk as a form of slower ('virtual') memory. Applications involving graphics or video tend to be more RAM-hungry, as do many 3D games or multimedia programs. The types and cost of memory are constantly changing; as a rule, RAM memory costs £1–£2 per megabyte and is normally available in 32, 64, 128, 256, 512 and 1,000Mb units. PCs from different manufacturers often use different types of memory depending on performance, motherboard architecture and cost. So before rushing out to buy new memory, you need to find out two important things.

What type of memory does your PC use?

Memory in new or recently made PCs is either SDRAM or DDR memory. The manufacturer of your machine can give you the information about your PC. If this assistance is not available, removing a memory module from your machine (open the chassis of the computer, find the PC memory slots – see example below – and pull out a module) and taking it to a local computer centre for identification is another option. Before removing memory, make sure you follow the anti-static precautions detailed on the left and on page 131. Do not mix SDRAM and DDR modules.

How many free memory slots are available?

PC memory sits in dedicated slots on the system motherboard. Each of these slots can accept one memory module, with the total amount of memory not exceeding the motherboard's upper limit. Most new PCs accept at least 1Gb of RAM, although more advanced systems can support up to 1.5Gb. Open the chassis of the computer, find the PC memory slots (see diagrams 2 and 3 opposite) and count how many free slots you have. You should also note if the memory module has chips on both sides, as it is always advisable to find memory that matches in this respect.

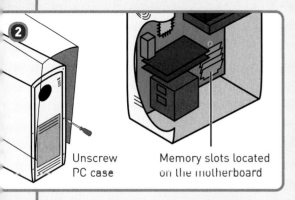

②

Unscrew
PC case

Memory slots located
on the motherboard

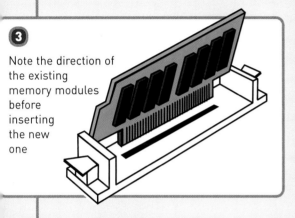

③

Note the direction of
the existing
memory modules
before
inserting
the new
one

④

Screw the case
back on to the PC

How to add RAM

1 Turn the power off at the mains and take anti-static precautions (see opposite margin).

2 Open the chassis and locate the free memory slots. These may be obscured by cables or the hard drive.

3 Locate the existing memory modules, match up the new memory in the same direction, slide the new module into the slot and click it into place. The memory will go in only one way. If you have to force it, try it the other way.

4 Secure the PC's chassis and reconnect the monitor, keyboard, mouse and power cables. Restart the system.

5 When the machine boots up it should automatically detect the new memory, providing an increased total. You can confirm this by right clicking on the **'My Computer'** icon within Windows and selecting **'Properties'**.

Memory management

Windows benefits greatly from memory upgrades. This is especially true of the recent versions such as 2000 and XP. There can be significant speed enhancements, and RAM upgrades have a long life. Most new PCs sold since 1998 use the same type of chips – 168-pin SDRAM DIMMS (dual inline memory modules). During 2000 manufacturers started moving to a faster type, called DDR (double data rate).

What to do if the upgrade does not work

Power down the system and open up the chassis. Make sure that all the memory modules are firmly in place. Then restart the computer.

If even that does not work, remove an existing memory module and put the new memory in its slot. Restart the system and see if the PC recognises the new memory. If it does, try the old memory in a slot directly adjacent to the new one. If the PC fails to recognise the old memory, you have memory of differing types and need to contact your memory supplier.

ADDING A HARD-DISK DRIVE

Before you start

Check your PC warranty. This task is quite time-consuming and there may be aspects of the design of your PC that affect the way an upgrade must be carried out. Most PC vendors provide experts on a technical support phone line to advise on such matters. If you are unsure, consult these experts before you begin.

Warning!

The main source of danger when working inside a PC is electricity. To protect yourself and your PC, take the following steps (see also page 131).

● Ensure the PC is still plugged in to the mains power but the wall socket is turned off.

● Touch the fingers of both hands on a metal part of the PC chassis to remove static electricity from your body before touching any components.

The software on your system resides on the hard disk. Most PC systems can hold more than one hard disk, thereby allowing you to store more software and data files. Hard-disk drives are getting progressively faster, such that new ones are often much faster than those made just a year or two previously. The detailed procedures for fitting a second hard-disk drive vary from one machine to the next. Follow the manufacturer's instructions in the context of this section's advice.

As computer applications (especially games) grow in size, you may need more space on your hard disk (see section 2.7). Instead of replacing your hard disk (see sections 6.8 and 6.9), you can add a second hard disk. But first make sure that the computer's chassis can support another drive.

● Open the chassis and find the existing hard disk, which will be located in a housing inside the PC secured by four screws. See if the chassis has an empty housing of a similar size which a second drive can fit into.

● Check whether the ribbon cable leading from the current hard drive to the motherboard has an additional plug on it, so it can connect to a second drive. If it does not, buy a new cable with a second connector in the middle (see diagram).

● Find out if you have enough power connectors free inside the chassis to support a second drive. Locate your existing hard drive and the power cable (see diagram), then find a matching unused cable. Also test that this power cable will reach your new hard disk. If you do not have a free power cable, buy an additional power cable splitter.

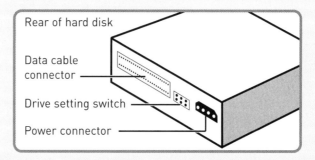

Rear of hard disk

Data cable connector

Drive setting switch

Power connector

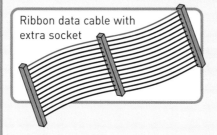

Ribbon data cable with extra socket

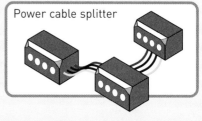

Power cable splitter

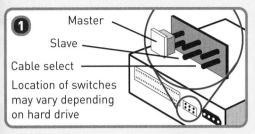

1. Master — Slave — Cable select — Location of switches may vary depending on hard drive

1 Following the steps in the manual for the new hard-disk drive, set the switches at the back (or underside) of the drive for use as a second drive. This is called 'slave' mode, as the second drive will be 'slaved' to the first.

Partitioning disks

Experienced users often partition large hard disks (over 20Mb in size) in order to organise programs and files. One can be used for Windows, another for applications, and yet another for data and documents. Note that you should normally partition a hard disk at the time of its installation. If you use FDISK to partition a disk already in use you will lose all of your data. Creating a new partition on an existing disk requires software like Partition Magic. Note that Windows 95 cannot support partitions larger than 2Mb – another good reason for moving on to later versions.

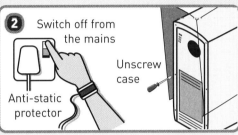

2. Switch off from the mains — Unscrew case — Anti-static protector

2 Turn the power off at the mains and take anti-static precautions (see margin).

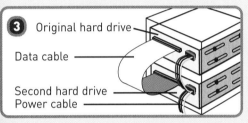

3. Original hard drive — Data cable — Second hard drive — Power cable

3 Open the chassis, fit the second drive into the free housing and secure with screws. Locate the existing hard disk and run the extra socket on the data cable to the new drive. Be sure to fit the power cable before closing and securing the chassis.

4 As your PC restarts, press the F8 (or F5) key to select either MS-DOS mode or safe mode with a command prompt, depending on your version of Windows. From this screen you can set up more than one virtual drive on each disk. Be careful not to create a partition on the C (i.e. original) drive (called 'drive 1') as you will erase all the information on it.

1 Normal
2 Logged
3 Safe mode
4 Step by step confirmation
5 Command prompt only
6 Safe mode command prompt only
7 Previous version of MSDOS

C:\fdisk

1. Create DOS partition or Logical DOS Drive
2. Set active partition
3. Delete partition or Logical DOS drive
4. Display partition information

5 To format the disk, type 'FORMAT (partition letter):'. The partition letter should generally be greater than E because A to D are normally used by floppy, hard disk and CD-ROM drives. Again, do not format the C drive as this is your original drive.

6 After the formatting is complete, reboot your PC. Windows should now list the new drive. Check this by double-clicking on the **'My Computer'** icon, which lists the available drives.

What to do if the new drive does not work

Check that the data and power cables are secured and the right way round. Try swapping the data cable around and go back to step 4 above. Look in the BIOS (see section 5.2) and make sure that the computer has auto-detected the new hard-disk drive. If not, you will need to enter the drive settings as detailed in the manual that came with the drive, or contact your supplier.

UPGRADING YOUR GRAPHICS SYSTEM

Before you start

Before you start to upgrade your graphics card, consult your PC warranty. There may be aspects of the design of your PC that affect the way an upgrade must be carried out. Most PC vendors provide experts on a technical support phone line to advise on such matters. If you are unsure, consult them before you begin.

Warning!

The main source of danger when working inside a PC is electricity. To protect yourself and your PC, take the following steps (see also page 131).

- Ensure the PC is still plugged in to the mains power but the wall socket is turned off.

- Touch the fingers of both hands on a metal part of the PC chassis to remove static electricity from your body before touching any components.

The deluge of 3D education, entertainment, design and games software means that graphics card technology can quickly fall from cutting-edge to run-of-the-mill. Replacing your graphics card with the most up-to-date version is a relatively easy task. Follow the manufacturer's instructions in the context of this section's advice.

There are two types of graphics system. Older PCs may use a PCI slot built in to the motherboard. The more common system has a special slot called the AGP (accelerated graphics port), designed only for graphics cards. On lower-cost or business-orientated PCs, the graphics features are embedded on to the motherboard. This makes the PC simpler to manufacture and set up, but hinders upgrading.

Before upgrading your video graphics system, decide what type of card best suits your needs and the constraints of your PC. AGP is to be preferred as it is faster. Some are designed for fast-paced, 3D video games, while others are more suited to video editing or CAD. Also, check what types of slots are available for your upgrade.

By accessing the Windows 'Properties' screen you can find many details about your graphics system before opening the chassis. Look for the amount of video RAM installed and the make and model of the card, to help you decide which type of card to upgrade to. More video memory can speed up performance of all graphic-intensive applications and games. Compare the make and model with another from the same supplier to ascertain what performance gain can be achieved.

To check that the new graphics card is suitable for your PC, open the chassis and locate your existing graphics system by tracing the monitor socket to either a plug-in card or the motherboard. If the graphics system is on the motherboard it probably cannot be upgraded. If the graphics system is on a card, find out if it uses an AGP or PCI slot. AGP slots are slightly smaller.

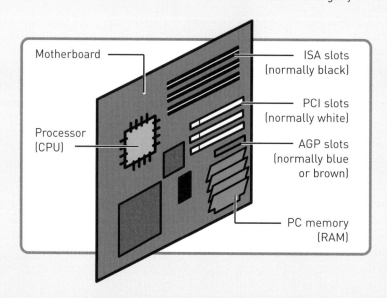

Motherboard

Processor (CPU)

ISA slots (normally black)

PCI slots (normally white)

AGP slots (normally blue or brown)

PC memory (RAM)

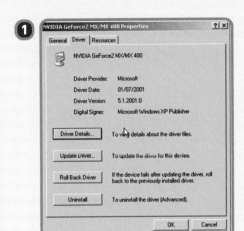

Upgrading a graphics card

1 Go into '**Control Panel**', '**System**' and '**Hardware**' and uninstall/remove the current graphics card.

2 Turn the power off at the mains and take anti-static precautions (see opposite margin).

3 Open the chassis and remove the existing graphics card. A single screw normally holds this in place.

More than a pretty picture

Many modern graphics cards are equipped for more than just PC images. A common feature is to allow television or video signals to be displayed on a PC screen while other applications are also running. This provision for video is also useful for video editing and playing DVD movie disks on your PC. Technically, if you watch TV on your PC screen you need a TV licence.

4 Insert the new card into the slot, making sure it is secure. If it will not slide in smoothly, check that the card matches the slot. Once inserted, screw the card into place and secure the chassis.

5 Reconnect all the cables and restart your PC. Windows should now detect a new graphics card and ask for the driver disk supplied by the graphics-card manufacturer. The system may need to restart before it will work with the new card.

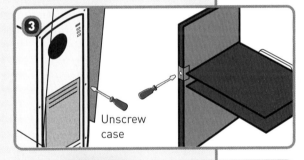

Unscrew case

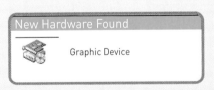

New Hardware Found

Graphic Device

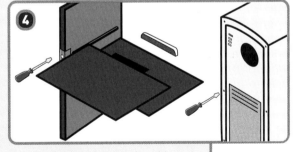

If you turn the computer back on after installing the new card and nothing appears on the screen:

- open the case and make sure that the card is seated securely
- make sure that the monitor cable is also securely fastened to the new graphics card output port
- if you have a graphics card built on to the motherboard, try connecting the monitor to this socket instead. If the display is still active, enter the BIOS (see section 5.2) and disable the onboard graphics.

REPLACING A CD-ROM DRIVE

Before you start

Check your PC warranty. Although the task itself is relatively easy, there may be aspects of the design of your PC that affect the way an upgrade must be carried out. Most PC vendors provide experts on a technical support phone line to advise on such matters. If you are unsure, consult these experts before you begin.

Warning!

The main source of danger when working inside a PC is electricity. To protect yourself and your PC, take the following steps (see also page 131).

- Ensure the PC is still plugged in to the mains power but the wall socket is turned off.

- Touch the fingers of both hands on a metal part of the PC chassis to remove static electricity from your body before touching any components.

Like any electromechanical device, a CD-ROM drive has a finite life span. This section shows how to test the drive on your PC. If you need to replace it, follow the manufacturer's instructions in the context of this section's advice.

New CD-ROM drives access data at up to 52 times the speed of earlier drives. To upgrade your CD-ROM drive, follow steps 1 to 9 below. If you believe that it has stopped working, try the following procedures before replacing it:

- make sure that the disk is the right way up and seated correctly
- use a CD-ROM disk which is known to work on another computer. If this disk works on your PC, it may be that you have a scratch on the disk you tried originally, not a faulty drive
- make sure that the device is listed in System Properties (see section 1.10) and that Windows believes it to be working
- play an audio disk. If this works it is more likely to be a software – rather than a hardware – problem
- clean the drive with a CD cleaner disk.

If after all these tests you find you need to replace the drive, you will need:

- a new internal IDE or SCSI (see Glossary) CD-ROM drive, or a combined DVD–CD-ROM drive. The former cost £25–£80 and are available from most computer stores. Most desktop PCs use IDE drives, but some powerful systems use SCSI drives
- CD-ROM driver software, which comes with new drives on a floppy disk. If you are buying a second-hand drive, make sure to ask the seller for the driver software disk. Drivers are available on the Internet but can be hard to locate.

How to install a CD-ROM drive

These installation steps cover IDE CD-ROMs as they are the more common type.

1 In Windows, go to the System Information (see section 1.10) screen and remove the old CD-ROM device. Then power the system down.

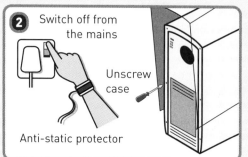

2 Switch off from the mains

Unscrew case

Anti-static protector

2 Turn the power off at the mains and take anti-static precautions (see margin).

3 Open the chassis and locate the cables which run from the motherboard to the rear of the CD-ROM drive. Remove the larger, ribbon-style cable from the back of the drive, taking note of which way up it fitted into the drive.

4 Trace the second, smaller cable which runs from the CD-ROM drive to the power supply. This power cable carries 12v and fits in only one way. Remove this cable from the back of the drive. The CD-ROM drive will be supplied with a thin cable. One end plugs into the appropriate socket on the drive and the other connects to your soundcard (or a marked connector on your PC's motherboard).

5 Locate and remove the screws holding the drive inside the 5-inch bay. There are normally four screws mounted at the side of the drive.

6 Slide the drive out through either the front or back of the bay, insert the replacement drive and affix screws to secure the new drive in the bay.

7 Insert the data and power cables into the back of the new drive. Make sure that both the notch and the red line are as they were on the original drive.

8 Place the lid back on the case and fix the screws back in place. Reconnect the power cable.

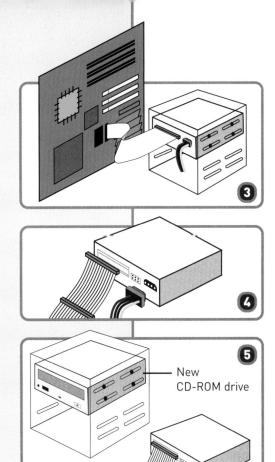

New CD-ROM drive

New Hardware Found   **9**

CD Rom Device

9 Restart the system. Windows should auto-detect the new hardware. It might ask for a driver disk, but this is unlikely. Your new CD-ROM drive will appear when you double-click on the **'My Computer'** icon.

How CD-ROMs work

The principle behind the working of a CD-ROM is quite simple. The surface of each disk has tiny reflective mirrors. The mirrors are arranged at an angle so that when a laser from the playing head strikes the mirrors, light is bounced to sensors on the left or the right. Each of these sensors represents a one or a zero, so the information can be represented in binary code.

What to do if the new drive does not work

Go back to step 7 and make sure the cables are securely connected, the right way round. Try the ribbon cable the other way (if it will fit). The drive will not be damaged if the data cable is placed the wrong way round. Make sure that the device is displayed under 'System Properties'.

REPLACING A FLOPPY-DISK DRIVE

Before you start

Check your PC warranty. Although the task itself is relatively easy, there may be aspects of the design of your PC that affect the way an upgrade must be carried out. Most PC vendors provide experts on a technical support phone line to advise on such matters. If you are unsure, consult these experts before you begin.

Warning!

The main source of danger when working inside a PC is electricity. To protect yourself and your PC, take the following steps (see also page 131).

- Ensure the PC is still plugged in to the mains power but the wall socket is turned off.

- Touch the fingers of both hands on a metal part of the PC chassis to remove static electricity from your body before touching any components.

Like any electromechanical device, a floppy-disk drive has a finite life span. This section shows how to test the drive on your PC and carry out simple repairs. If the drive is beyond repair, you need to replace it. Follow the manufacturer's instructions in the context of this section's advice.

The $3\frac{1}{2}$-inch-floppy-disk drive is found in most desktop PCs. If you believe that the drive on your PC has stopped working, try the following:

- use a disk from another computer
- make sure that the write-protect tab (on the top right-hand corner) is correctly positioned. You can save files on to the disk only if this tab is in the closed position. The tab protects files from accidental deletion
- buy a fresh set of blank $3\frac{1}{2}$-inch disks and try formatting them
- make sure your anti-virus software is up-to-date
- make sure that the floppy disk is listed in the POST screen when the PC first starts up.

If after all these tests you find you need to replace the drive, you will need a new floppy-disk drive. These cost under £20.

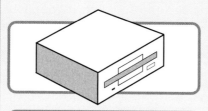

Switch off from the mains

Anti-static protector

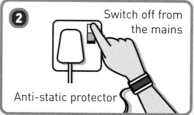

Unscrew case

How to install a floppy-disk drive

1 In Windows, go to the 'System Information' (see section 1.10) screen and remove the old floppy-disk device. Then power the system down.

2 Turn the power off at the mains and take anti-static precautions (see margin).

3 Open the chassis, locate the cables which run from the computer's motherboard and power-supply unit to the rear of the floppy-disk drive. Remove the larger ribbon-style data cable from the back of the floppy disk drive, taking note of which way up it fitted into the drive. To help you, most cables have a red line down one side and a notch on the top of the plastic connector.

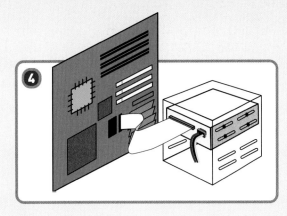

4 Trace the second, smaller cable which runs from the floppy-disk drive to the power supply. This power cable fits in only one way. Remove this cable from the back of the drive.

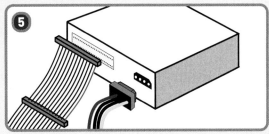

5 Locate and remove the screws holding the floppy-disk drive inside the 3½-inch bay. There are normally four screws mounted at the side of the drive.

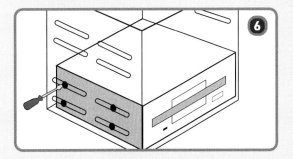

6 Slide the drive out through either the front or back of the bay, insert the replacement drive and affix screws to secure the new drive in the bay.

How floppy disks work

A floppy-disk drive works on a similar principle to a cassette player but uses magnetic properties instead of grooves and pits. A magnetic sensor (read head) moves over the surface of the disk looking for patterns of magnetically charged areas to determine stored information. The opposite happens when storing information – a small magnet (write head) changes the magnetic field on parts of the disk depending on the information it needs to save.

7 Insert the floppy-drive data cable into the back of the new drive. Make sure that both the notch and the red line are as they were when the original drive was installed. Insert the power cable, taking care not to force either cable.

8 Place the lid back on the case and fix the screws back in place. Reconnect the power cable and test your new floppy-disk drive.

What to do if the new drive does not work

If the floppy-drive activity light is permanently on or no light comes on when you try to access the drive, go back to step 7 and make sure the data cable is connected the right way round and securely attached. Try the cable the other way (if it will fit). The drive will not be damaged if the data cable is placed the wrong way round.

Go into the PC's BIOS (see section 5.2) and make sure that the 3½-inch floppy-disk drive is listed and is set to the 1.44Mb mode.

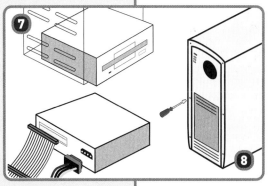

Warning!

Make sure that no foreign objects, such as coins, have been forced into the drive slot by inexperienced users or children, or that the shutter has not come off a disk and stayed inside. This can stop the floppy-disk drive from working.

UPGRADING YOUR SOUND SYSTEM

Before you start

Before you start to upgrade your soundcard, consult the terms of your PC warranty. There may be aspects of the design of your PC that affect the way an upgrade must be carried out. Most PC vendors provide experts on a technical support phone line to advise on such matters. If you are unsure, consult them before you begin.

Warning!

The main source of danger when working inside a PC is electricity. To protect yourself and your PC, take the following steps (see also page 131).

- Ensure the PC is still plugged in to the mains power but the wall socket is turned off.

- Touch the fingers of both hands on a metal part of the PC chassis to remove static electricity from your body before touching any components.

The soundcard is an incredibly reliable part of the PC system. If you are a keen musician, you may want to upgrade the soundcard to one more suited to your creative endeavour. Although this is a relatively simple task, integrating the new card into a complete multimedia system is more complex. Follow the manufacturer's instructions in the context of this section's advice.

Many PCs now come with a built-in soundcard. Budget soundcards, although adequate for multimedia, are of limited use for musicians or for surround sound. On lower-cost or business-orientated PCs, many manufacturers embed the sound features directly on to the motherboard. This makes the PC simpler to manufacture and set up, but hinders upgrading.

Before upgrading your soundcard, find out what type of card best suits your needs and the constraints of your PC. Some soundcards offer features such as extra memory for holding extended MIDI samples or a port able to accept digital input from other audio devices. You also need to identify physically what type of slots are available for your soundcard upgrade.

Using the Windows Properties screen (see section 1.10) you can find many details about your sound system before opening the chassis. The main features to look for are the amount of RAM available for MIDI and the make and model of the existing soundcard. This information can help you decide which type of soundcard to upgrade to. Having extra MIDI RAM memory is useful for musicians. Comparing the make and model with others from the same supplier helps to ascertain which features will be available after upgrading to a newer model.

To make sure that the new soundcard is suitable for your PC, open the chassis and locate your existing sound system by tracing the speaker socket to either a plug-in card or the motherboard. If the sound sub-system is on the motherboard it is very unlikely that this can be upgraded without disabling it in BIOS (see section 5.2). If the sound system is on a card, you need to find out if it uses an ISA or PCI slot (the former is much longer than the latter). The diagram on page 136 should help.

If you have decided to upgrade your soundcard and the existing card is built in to the PC's motherboard, you must disable it before your new sound hardware will work correctly. To do this you need to do two things:

- remove the device from your System Properties (see section 1.10)
- enter the BIOS (see section 5.2) and disable the soundcard located under the Sound, Video and Game Controllers section of the System Properties.

How to upgrade your soundcard

1 When you have bought a new soundcard and are ready to install it, first go into **'System Properties'** (see section 1.10) in Windows and remove the existing sound driver. Then power the system down.

2 Turn the power off at the mains and take anti-static precautions (see opposite margin).

3 Open the chassis and remove the existing soundcard. A single screw normally holds this in place.

4 Insert the new card into an appropriate slot, making sure it is firmly seated. If it will not slide in smoothly, check that the card matches the slot. Once it is inserted, screw the card into place and secure the chassis.

5 Reconnect all the cables including those to the speakers and to the CD-ROM drive and restart your PC. Windows should now detect a new soundcard and ask for the driver disk supplied by the soundcard manufacturer. The system may need to restart after this but once restarted should work with the new soundcard.

What to do if the new soundcard does not work

If you turn the computer back on after installing the new card and the soundcard does not work:

- open the case and make sure that the card is seated securely
- make sure that the speaker cable is also securely fastened to the new soundcard output port
- if you have a soundcard built on to the motherboard, try your speakers in the old speaker sockets. Play a sound on your PC: if the old sound system is still active, you need to enter the BIOS (see section 5.2) and disable the onboard sound
- have a look at the section on sound troubleshooting (section 4.10).

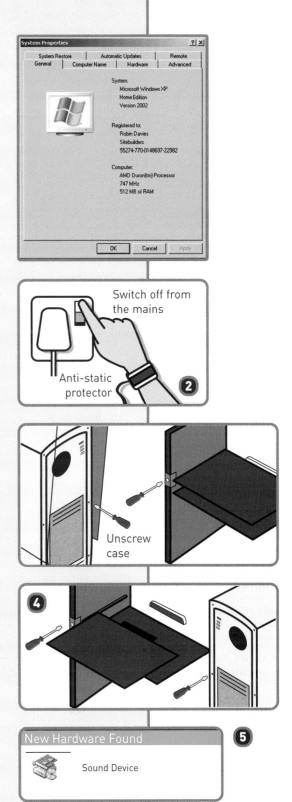

6 | Upgrading and replacing hardware

143

UPGRADING YOUR MODEM

Before you start

Before you start to upgrade your modem, consult the terms of your PC warranty. There may be aspects of the design of your PC that affect the way an upgrade must be carried out. Most PC vendors provide experts on a technical support phone line to advise on such matters. If you are unsure, consult them before you begin.

Warning!

The main source of danger when working inside a PC is electricity. To protect yourself and your PC, take the following steps (see also page 131).

● Ensure the PC is still plugged in to the mains power but the wall socket is turned off.

● Touch the fingers of both hands on a metal part of the PC chassis to remove static electricity from your body before touching any components.

A modem is a device (connected using a telephone line) used to surf the Internet, access emails and send and receive faxes. It may be external or internal. Upgrading an external modem simply involves buying a new one and plugging it in; upgrading an internal one is harder. Follow the manufacturer's instructions in the context of this section's advice.

Many new PCs are supplied with a modem. Some have an internal card modem while more recent PCs have a modem built into the motherboard. The latter hinders upgrading, but if it conforms to the V90 standard (check your PC's documentation) that will not be a problem. Some modems offer extra facilities, such as sending and receiving faxes or acting as an answerphone. These facilities can often be available even when your PC is switched off.

There is a new modem standard called V92. This became available in modems during 2001. It offers three new facilities: **'QuickConnect'**, **'Modem-on-Hold'** and **'PCM Upstream'**. While the virtues of **'QuickConnect'** are fairly obvious, **'Modem-on-Hold'** is potentially very useful for those users with only one telephone line: it allows you to receive an incoming call and stay connected to the Internet (a call-waiting service from your phone company is all that is required). It also works in reverse; you can initiate a voice call while connected and keep the modem connection. **'PCM Upstream'** speeds the transmission of data to your ISP.

Using the Windows 'Properties' screen (see section 1.10) you can find many details about your modem before opening the chassis. Some modems plug directly into the serial ports of your PC and are the easiest to upgrade. At the moment the fastest speed for modems using a normal telephone line is 56K.

To make sure that the new modem is suitable for your PC, open the chassis and locate your existing modem by tracing the telephone cable slot to either a plug-in card or the motherboard. If the modem is on the motherboard it is very unlikely that this can be upgraded. If the modem is on a card, you need to find out if it uses an ISA or PCI slot (the former is much longer than the latter). The diagram below should help.

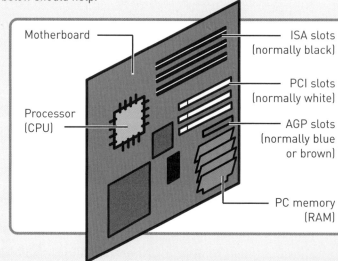

Motherboard —
Processor (CPU) —
ISA slots (normally black)
PCI slots (normally white)
AGP slots (normally blue or brown)
PC memory (RAM)

How to upgrade your modem

1 When you have bought a new modem and are ready to install it, first go into **'System Properties'** (see section 1.10) in Windows and remove the existing modem. Then power down the system.

2 Turn off the power at the mains and take anti-static precautions (see opposite margin).

3 Open the chassis and remove the existing modem card. A single screw normally holds this in place.

4 Insert the new card into the previously occupied slot, making sure it is firmly seated. If it will not slide in smoothly, check that the card matches the slot. Once it is inserted, screw the card into place and secure the chassis.

5 Reconnect all the cables and restart your PC. Windows should now detect a new modem and ask for the driver disk supplied by the modem manufacturer. The system may need to restart after this, but once restarted should work with the new modem.

6 Any application that uses the modem may need to have its settings changed to point to the new modem.

What to do if the new modem does not work

If you turn the computer back on after installing the new card and the modem does not work:

● open the case and make sure that the card is seated securely
● make sure that the telephone cable is in the correct slot. If your modem has two sockets for a telephone jack, try making a telephone call with an attached handset. If you cannot, switch the cables round
● if you have a modem built on to the motherboard, try the telephone lead in this slot instead. If it still works you need to enter the BIOS (see section 5.2) and disable the onboard modem
● look at the sections on Internet troubleshooting (section 7.6).

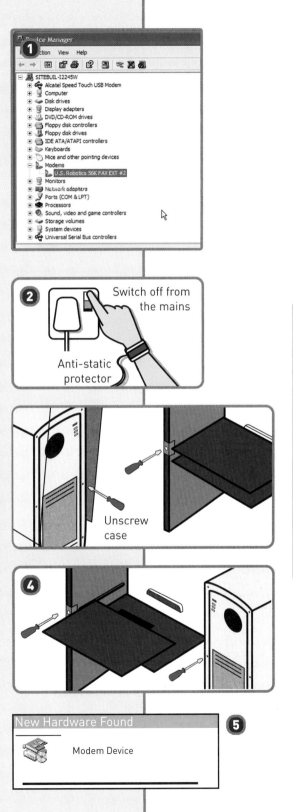

REPLACING A HARD-DISK DRIVE (I)

Before you start

Replacing a hard disk is a complex job because many of the pre-installed applications and settings may be available only from the original PC manufacturer. Before you start to replace the hard disk, consult the terms of your PC warranty.

Warning!

The main source of danger when working inside a PC is electricity. To protect yourself and your PC, take the following steps (see also page 131).

- **Ensure the PC is still plugged in to the mains power but the wall socket is turned off.**

- **Touch the fingers of both hands on a metal part of the PC chassis to remove static electricity from your body before touching any components.**

Hard-disk drives are mechanical, not electronic, devices and eventually wear out through use. Although the death of a hard drive does not mean you need a new PC, replacing the drive is a complex task. Follow the manufacturer's instructions in the context of the advice in this section and the next.

If you have a consistent backup strategy (see section 2.3), the failure of a hard disk is an annoyance but not a major catastrophe. Generally, hard disks die gradually. You may notice that files become corrupt, then, as this gets worse, one day the drive will fail to start up. However, you should note that if you turn your system on and it fails to start, it may not mean that the hard disk has failed. A critical file used at start-up might have been damaged and need replacing. Before throwing away your hard disk, run these tests:

- try using a boot disk (see section 2.3) to access the drive via DOS. If the drive is functioning correctly (i.e., you can see a C:\ prompt) it may mean that Windows needs to be fixed and that a new drive is not needed

- make sure that no floppies or CD-ROMS are in the PC at boot-up

- if you have anti-virus software, try running it from a clean boot disk (most anti-virus software asks you to create a boot or emergency floppy during installation). Some of the nastier viruses can prevent a PC from starting correctly

- check the PC's BIOS (see section 5.2) and make sure that the hard disk is listed correctly

- open the case and make sure that the power and data cables have not been detached from the hard disk

- try running ScanDisk.

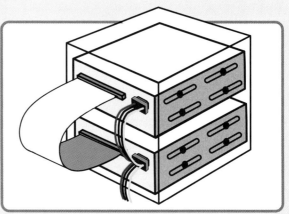

If after these tests you still find you need to replace the drive, you will need:

- a new internal hard disk. These cost between £60 and £200. They range in size from 20Gb to 180Gb for an IDE drive

- Windows software on CD-ROM.

Do not throw away your old hard drive. After you have installed the new one, you can temporarily hook up the old one. If you are able read the old drive, you could transfer documents to the new drive.

How to replace a hard-disk drive

1 Turn the power off at the mains and take anti-static precautions (see margin on facing page).

2 Open the chassis, locate and remove the existing hard disk, and place the new hard disk in the same drive mount. Make sure that both the power and data cables are as they were when the old drive was in place.

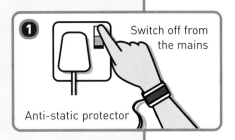

Switch off from the mains

Anti-static protector

3 Some computer systems allow you to boot up straight from a CD-ROM disk. To test if yours can, place your Windows CD-ROM in the drive and power the system up. If the Windows set-up program runs, follow the on-screen instructions. If, after you insert the Windows installation CD, the system fails to perform the set-up procedure, you will have to set up the disk manually. See next section.

4 If Windows does install automatically, you may find that it asks you to install various device drivers for items such as the soundcard, modem and printer. These are normally provided with the PC on either floppy disks or CD. If you do not have these disks, contact your PC manufacturer.

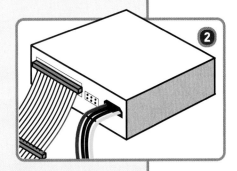

What to do if the new drive does not work

You may not have a bootable CD-ROM drive (see point 3 above). Make sure that the settings in the BIOS (see section 5.2) are set for booting first from a CD-ROM. Make sure all cables are securely fitted and are the right way round.

REPLACING A HARD-DISK DRIVE (II)

This section is to be read after the previous one. If your PC cannot boot up from a CD-ROM, you need to follow the instructions in this section to complete the installation of your hard disk. Again, follow the manufacturer's instructions in the context of this section's advice.

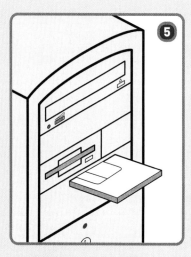

How to replace a hard-disk drive (continued)

5 If your PC is not capable of booting up from a CD-ROM, you need to initialise the new hard-disk drive using a bootable floppy disk. (For information on making a bootable floppy disk see section 2.3). Turn the PC off, place the boot disk in the floppy-disk drive and turn the PC on again.

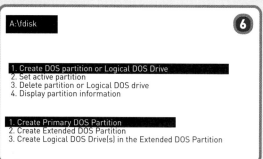

6 After the PC has booted up from the floppy disk, A:\ appears on the screen. At this point you need to partition and format the disk. To set a partition, type **'FDISK'** and follow the on-screen instructions to create a single DOS partition. From this screen you can set up more than one virtual drive on each disk. These partitions each have a unique letter identifying them. However, the main partition (or boot partition) must be the C: drive.

7 Next, format the disk to allow Windows to be installed. You need to type **'FORMAT C: /S'** and follow the on-screen prompts. You will need to format extra partitions separately for Windows to recognise them. To do this, type in **'FORMAT'** (partition letter): but you do not need to type the '/S' syntax, which copies the system files on to the drive. Next, reboot your PC – the system should now boot up without the aid of a floppy disk, and end up with a C:\ prompt on the screen.

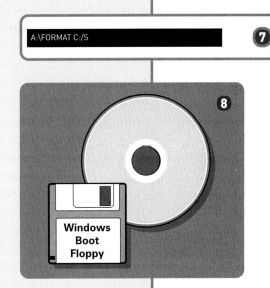

A:\FORMAT C:/S **7**

Windows
Boot
Floppy

8 Windows XP CDs are bootable and you should not need a boot floppy. However, if your system will not boot from the CD-ROM you will need to boot from a floppy or use a floppy-based installation as mentioned in section 2.3. If the CD boots, the XP installation process will begin automatically and it is largely a question of following the on-screen prompts. Go to step (10). If your CD will not boot, go to step (9).

9 Although most PCs built in the past few years will boot from Windows CDs, there are occasions when this will not work. If your CD will not boot, you will have to use a floppy-installation process. Refer to the end of section 2.3 for information on how to create these floppies. You may have to create these floppies on another PC. The installation process is the same as using a bootable Windows CD, but much slower at the beginning.

10 Once you have installed Windows on your new hard disk, you will need to restore your document files and re-install your applications.

What to do if the new drive does not work

If your drive does not work, test that all the cables are securely attached and that the BIOS (see section 5.2) has correctly recognised the new drive.

FAQS ON UPGRADING

Upgrading a PC can give rise to queries and problems. Here are some of the most commonly asked questions and some possible solutions.

If I upgrade my PC, will it invalidate my warranty?
In 99 per cent of cases, no. However, occasionally some companies that sell PCs insist that any upgrades are carried out with them because the machine contains non-standard parts (or because it was sold to you under a special deal). If this is the case, you should have been informed of it when you bought your PC.

What can I do with my old parts after an upgrade?
Your best bet is a private sale. With hardware components priced extremely competitively, few companies buy anything other than complete systems. Do not expect to retire on the proceeds.

Is buying via the Internet or mail order a good idea?
Yes. You can save a great deal of money buying online or through magazine adverts. However, there is usually a delivery charge and if what you buy is not suitable, faulty or incompatible, you will have to pay to return the item unless you can prove the supplier was at fault.

The company which sold me my PC has gone bust. Where can I get repairs?
Most PCs use standard components that are widely available from any PC repair or service company. If you need a repair or upgrade, quote the make and model of the PC and get confirmation that the company is able to service your machine before you send any cash.

My laptop is faulty. Can I repair it myself?
Laptops use specialised parts that are far more difficult to repair or replace than those of standard PCs. Even opening a laptop without proper training could dislodge sensitive components. Contact the manufacturer for a list of authorised repair centres and use one of them instead.

Can I upgrade my monitor's performance?
Unfortunately not. If you decide to buy a new monitor, keep the older one as a spare as monitors tend to hold their value and are a useful basis for building a second system.

My PC appears to be getting slower the more I use it. Is this possible?
Yes, in a way. The PC is probably performing at the same speed but you may have loaded more applications such as anti-virus programs, electronic address books, colourful wallpaper, screen savers and the like, which all take up a bit of memory. You can download free 'benchmarking' software to test the performance of your PC, and you can retest your PC's benchmark whenever you want to make sure your machine is not slowing down in any way. Adding extra RAM can enhance performance significantly and is a simple upgrade. See section 6.1.

I play a lot of games that run o.k. – but only at low resolution. How can I improve the images?
You probably need a more powerful video card with at least 32Mb of RAM and which handles 3D and 2D graphics comfortably. Prices start at £40. You would also benefit from a larger monitor. Today, a 17-inch screen is seen as a minimum.

I've upgraded a device and now another device has stopped working. What shall I do?
This is quite common. Many of the devices in your PC rely on one another. Try removing the affected device from your Windows system settings (see section 1.10), then restart your PC. When your PC starts it will try to join the two devices together so they can communicate again. To avoid conflict, install one of the devices in a different slot. If this fails, you may need to contact the hardware manufacturer of the new device you have bought.

I want to upgrade my PC but I've run out of slots to put new devices in. What can I do?
This is a very common problem. The easiest way is to buy external versions of the devices you want to add, e.g. use an external modem or network card instead of the slots inside your machine. If this is not possible, you may be able to buy devices that do more than one job but take up only one slot, e.g. a soundcard with built-in modem or graphics card with a built-in video capture card.

I'm running out of hard-disk space for my documents. What can I do?
You have two main options. You could buy a second hard disk and fit this into your machine, which requires some technical savvy (see sections 6.8 and 6.9). Another option would be to use a removable device such as a CD writer, tape backup or Zip disk and move your infrequently used files to removable media: this option is easiest but moving files can be slow and the cost of some types of media quite high. You could try compressing your hard disk (see section 2.7).

My keyboard [or mouse] is sluggish or temperamental. What can I do?
Keyboards and mice are not as durable as many computer components and are exposed to dirt and grime. Try cleaning your mouse or keyboard with a computer cleaning kit. Even if you do this regularly, expect to have to replace them after a few years.

For many people Internet access, for education, entertainment, communication and e-commerce, is a key reason for owning a PC. The number of new Internet users is growing apace and the desktop PC is the catalyst for this growth. The modern PC can be used to send and receive pictures (live or static), documents, files, faxes and other data. The humble modem plays a key role in each one of these tasks and as such is vital for anybody wanting to join the information super highway. Not only can the modem connect to the Internet but it can also send and receive facsimiles without the need for paper.

For most home users, the telephone is the simplest and most cost-effective way to communicate with other computers. It is fairly slow, but also quite cheap (if you are careful). This is changing with the gradual spread of broadband facilities offered by cable modems and ADSL. These much faster services operate for a fixed monthly fee.

To use any of the data services available via the telephone, you will need a modem. Most modern PCs incorporate a modem, but if yours does not, fitting one is reasonably straightforward (see section 6.7).

The main problems associated with the Internet are of compatibility and reliability. The Internet, for all its wonders, can still be painfully slow. New standards and applications appear on an almost daily basis, each with its own benefits and related problems.

Security is also a big concern — not only in the context of buying online but also because so much undesirable, even harmful, content is widely available on the web. Viruses, illegal software and pornography all make the web a place in which to tread with caution. Computer systems and users can be protected from these pitfalls by low-cost or even free software, some of which is built into Windows.

This section explains how to set up your system for the Internet and fix the most common problems that you are likely to encounter.

COMMUNICATION, NETWORKING AND THE INTERNET

7 | Communication, networking and the Internet

CONNECTING TO THE INTERNET

ISP or online service?

Unless you are a government, university or very large business, you cannot connect your computer directly to the Internet. Instead, you have to use a third party to do so.

Two types of company exist to do this – Internet service providers (ISPs) and online service providers (OSPs). ISPs offer a connection to the Internet for either a monthly fee (which may include a free telephone number to dial up to connect) or for no charge other than telephone calls to a local-rate number. You are provided with a no-frills connection to the Net and, often, an email address. OSPs, such as AOL, CompuServe or Which? Online, require a monthly subscription, but offer substantial proprietary content which can be accessed only by subscribers. This extra content may include built-in parental controls, online games, email and storage space for your website. The boundaries between ISPs and OSPs have blurred in the past few years and it is a constantly changing situation.

The Internet is now part of everyday life for many PC users. Many companies offer Internet connections and services. This section explains how the Internet works and what types of connection are available.

Getting online

Every Internet service provider offers you a CD-ROM to help you connect to the Internet. This CD-ROM contains all the settings and software, such as browsers, that you need to sign up. You simply follow the instructions that come with the CD-ROM and within ten minutes you can be online.

Many services are free. They normally include a number of email addresses that you can create and some space for hosting your own home web page. Often the difference between a free service and a paid-for service is the number of extra features your ISP offers. These include multiple access points around the world – so, if you are abroad, you can retrieve your email by dialling a local number; free online games; reference material; and better technical support on Internet matters.

Also, free providers are unlikely to support faster-connection technologies such as ISDN, cable modems or ADSL.

Modem If you connect to the Internet from home, your computer probably uses a modem. The word derives from modulator-demodulator, and the device translates computer information into a form which can be transmitted over an ordinary telephone line.

Modems supplied with new PCs or purchased since 2000 should conform to the V90 standard established by the International Telecommunications Union. A new standard, V92, emerged in 2001, but as of January 2002, only one ISP in the UK supported it. See section 6.7 for details.

ISDN In effect a digital telephone line, ISDN (integrated services digital network) offers you a minimum connection speed of 64Kbits/sec to your ISP. However, because all ISDN installations include at least two lines (known as channels) you can combine these to give an effective access speed of 128Kbits/sec or even more.

The installation cost of ISDN is high, and if you want speeds above 64Kbits/sec you will be charged for making two or more access calls simultaneously. However, the connection time for each call is much quicker on a digital line (typically five seconds, compared to 45 or so using a modem), and as long as you have a free channel you can make voice calls even while you are on the Net.

GSM, GPRS and WAP (mobile phones) It is possible to connect to the Internet using a digital mobile phone: all those sold in the UK currently use the GSM standard. However, the speed of connection is very slow so Web-surfing is extremely tedious. New 3G mobile technologies will soon make connections faster, but in the meantime it is best to reserve GSM connections for quickly checking your email.

To connect via a mobile phone, you need a phone handset which can make data as well as voice calls. Some include a GSM modem: if yours does not, you will also need a modem card which can connect to your phone. You will also need a cable or infrared link.

ADSL (broadband) BT launched ADSL (asymmetrical digital subscriber line) in the autumn of 1999 and has since rolled out the service to a number of areas in the UK. In January 2002 BT claimed to serve areas where some 70 per cent of Internet users live. The reality is that if you live in an urban area, you may have a good chance of ADSL provision eventually. Rural areas have no provision and are unlikely to for some years. During 2002 BT plans to trial broadband by satellite for rural areas. It is likely to be expensive. ADSL allows your computer to be connected to the Internet permanently. Although it uses the same wires as your phone line, you pay a fixed, monthly fee (currently £39.99 including VAT) for an always-on connection at 512Kbits/sec. Voice calls can be made at the same time and normal charges apply to those.

Cable modem The two main cable companies in the UK, Telewest and NTL, offer broadband provision through cable modems. The service is similar to ADSL, although somewhat cheaper. Again, like BT's ADSL, the service is confined to urban areas where cable services have been installed.

LAN (local area network) You are most likely to encounter a LAN at work. It is used to connect several computers together, allowing their users to share files with each other and access common resources such as printers and scanners. However, the LAN may also be connected to the Internet. In this case, it allows all the attached computers to access the Net as well. As the LAN is likely to be connected to an expensive but speedy leased line or using several ISDN channels, Internet access using it will be rapid.

The Web is the Internet

The Internet is the generic term for the worldwide network of interlinked computers to which you connect whenever you dial into your ISP. Conceived in 1969, as the American military's ARPAnet, a system for the exchange of scientific information, it was joined by other organisations, mainly universities and research agencies, in the 1970s and 80s. Thereafter, it became publicly accessible.

The Web, a comparatively recent development, is the most accessible part of the Internet. It uses protocols developed at the CERN research labs (and credited to the Englishman Tim Berners-Lee) to make the information stored on the Net accessible using graphical browsers.

Usenet, better known as Newsgroups, is a further subset of the Internet: it allows fast text-only discussion forums to thrive. And the most common application of all, email, relies on Internet-connected computers to transmit messages.

THE INTERNET BROWSER

Dot what?

The suffix in a web address (.com; .org.; .net; .co.uk) fall into two groups. Generic Top Level Domains (gTLDs) are .com; .net; .org; edu; .int; .mil; and .gov. Originating in the USA, they refer to, respectively, a commercial body, a non-profit making organisation, an ISP, an educational establishment, an organisation established by international treaty, the US military and the US government. The first three of these are commercial domains and can be registered by anybody. The remainder are restricted.

gTLDs are followed by country-code TLDs (ccTLDs). An example is those belonging to the UK, such as .co.uk or .org.uk. Each country has a two-letter code. Note that domains might well be registered in a specific country, but are often hosted elsewhere. A site which explains all this in great detail is the Internet Corporation for Assigned Names and Numbers (ICANN) at www.icann.org

The most common Internet browser is Microsoft's Internet Explorer. Version 6 is supplied with Windows XP. Other browsers are Netscape (used by 7 to 10 per cent of Internet users worldwide) and Opera (used by a smaller number). This section explains the basics of the Internet Explorer interface.

1 Menu options

2 Go to previous page

3 If you have already gone back a page, this will take you forward a page

4 'Stop' aborts the loading of the current page

5 If a page is not displaying correctly, 'Refresh' will attempt to load the page again

6 Clicking on 'Home' will launch the default start page for your browser. This can be changed via the options described in the next section

7 'Search' will launch the default search tools for finding items on the Internet

8 Internet site address

9 Links to other web pages are either underlined, in a different colour

(typically blue), or change colour as you pass the mouse pointer over them. Clicking on them takes you to the linked item, which may be on the same site or on a different site

10 This bar provides information on what the browser is currently doing. If you leave the mouse over a link, it will also give you some information on where that link will take you

11 A bar in the bottom centre of the browser window represents the loading of the page

12 Calls up a list of your favourite sites. To add (or 'bookmark') sites click on **'Favorites'** on the top toolbar

13 **'History'** stores a list of websites you have been to over the last few weeks

14 Clicking on **'Fullscreen'** toggles the browser between the standard view and a special mode that hides a lot of the menus and buttons.

Moving the mouse to the top of the screen brings back some of the options and allows you to toggle back to the standard mode

15 Clicking on **'Mail'** launches the default mail program

16 Clicking on **'Print'** triggers the printing of the current web page

17 If you have compatible web publishing software,

the **'Edit'** icon may appear. This allows you to grab the page for editing

18 Many websites have a search facility on them. In this example, typing a word and clicking on **'Go'** starts a search of the entire BBC website for instances of the word typed. When a match is found, another click will take you to the relevant page

Storing images from the Net

By right-clicking on a picture on a website then selecting **'Save As'**, you can store images from the Net on your PC. However, if you decide to republish any of these images you must first obtain permission from the website's owner.

Warning!

When buying goods over the Internet, use a credit card. Most credit-card companies now offer protection schemes for goods bought over the Net and which include insurance against fraud. Contact your credit-card company for more details. Ensure you buy from a trusted site (look for the Which? Web Trader or TrustUK logos) and check that it is secure (a padlock will be displayed at the bottom of the screen).

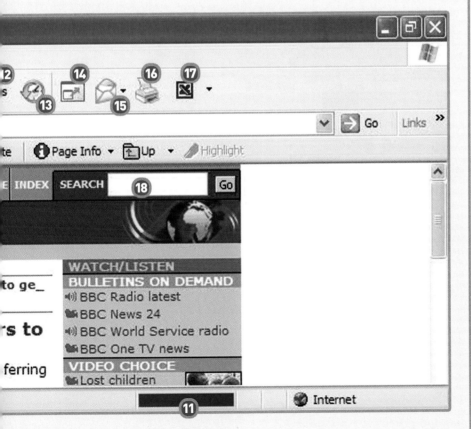

BROWSER OPTIONS

Other types of browsers

Netscape was first in the market with a working and popular browser. Microsoft then produced Internet Explorer (IE) and bundled it with Windows. Netscape quickly lost market share and, despite legal action by the US government which forced Microsoft to allow Windows XP to work without the installation of IE, most users on the Internet now use IE. Netscape has recently fought back and with version 6 released a credible alternative to IE. Another well-regarded browser is Opera. This is small and fast, offering excellent facilities. Despite the enthusiasm of a devoted band of fans, Opera has a very low user base.

For users of services such as CompuServe or AOL, the browser is a special version for use only with that service. These browsers normally come with extensive help files and additional features such as parental protection and service-specific email accounts.

Configuring your browser for general operation and managing security is essential for safe and happy web surfing. The main Internet Explorer options can be found under Tools/Internet Options from the main menu bar.

1 You can change your home page via this option. This is the page that the software loads up first, each time you connect to the Internet

2 Temporary files can take up quite a bit of hard-disk space but improve the loading speed of frequently used websites. By clicking on settings, you can alter how much hard-disk space is used for temporary files. The **'Delete Files'** option removes temporary files, freeing up hard-disk space

3 By increasing the number of days kept in the history file, you can find web pages you visited some time ago by clicking on the **'History'** button within your browser. For security or privacy you may, however, want to keep your history and temporary file folder short

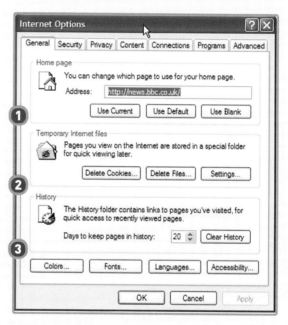

The four options along the bottom, Colors, Fonts, Languages and Accessibility, control how Internet Explorer and web pages are displayed. For the most part these options are rarely touched. However, they are quite self-explanatory, allowing you to change default colours, fonts and preferred languages. The accessibility options are designed to improve legibility for partially sighted users.

Internet Explorer has a number of pre-set security options, arranged under a scheme called 'zones'. However, for home users the Internet is treated as a single zone called the **'Internet zone'**. Zones are used in a business environment and you have a different security model depending whether you are connecting to a website hosted within your company or an external one.

The different default security settings range from low to high. On the lowest setting, many types of Internet content such as web-based applications and documents are automatically loaded and executed. Also, details about your computer and your user information are transmitted without warning across the Internet. On the highest setting, every time non-standard content is about to be downloaded, the browser will give you the option of refusing it. Also, information about you is withheld or confirmation is required before this information is sent across the Internet.

Internet Explorer version 6 introduced a new Privacy setting in Tools/Options which allows you to decide how cookies should be handled. (See section 7.7 for information about cookies).

The other options within Internet Explorer are Content, Connection, Programs and Advanced.

Content contains information about you and tools for screening out undesirable sites. Unfortunately, the built-in content-screening software is not effective as the system has only a tiny number of sites which have been rated. Third-party products can be bought to protect children from viewing explicit websites (see section 3.10). Although these cost extra, they are far superior to the built-in protection software.

Connection is useful only if you have more than one connection to the Internet. From here, you can select which connection to establish. For example, if you have a Freeserve and a Demon account, you can select which one to access via this option.

Programs lists the default programs that will be launched if you click on the email or news icons within your browser.

Advanced lists over 40 options for tweaking your browser. Pressing F1 on this screen gives you more information on the tweaks you can make to the operation of your browser.

Upgrade to heaven

Newer versions of popular Internet browsers are constantly becoming available. Before you upgrade, write down the settings you need to set up your connection manually, in case the automatic upgrade procedure fails. This information is found under the Connection tab. Don't change anything, but instead write down your login details, password, connection types, access telephone number and any other pertinent information.

The current version of Internet Explorer is version 6, but the most widespread version in use is the 5.x series.

TYPICAL EMAIL SOFTWARE

There are many email programs, of which Outlook Express is the most popular as it comes with an installation of Internet Explorer. Its big brother, Outlook, is part of the Office suite. A popular alternative to Outlook is Eudora. An Internet search for free email clients will provide you with a list of suitable programs for all versions of Windows. This section looks at Outlook/Outlook Express.

1 Compose a new email message

2 Reply to a message in your Inbox

3 Reply to a message which has been sent to you as part of a group. With this command you can reply to everyone on the same distribution list

4 Forward a message to another email address

5 'Send and Receive' attempts to connect to your ISP, send any email waiting in the Outbox and collect any email waiting for you at your ISP

6 Use this to delete a message

7 These are the emails currently residing within this folder (in this case, your Inbox)

8 List of possible folders where emails can reside. By right-clicking on the **'Outlook Express'** icon and selecting **'New Folder'** you can create your own filing system for emails

9 You can store details of people you email within the **'Address Book'**. If you receive an email, double-click on it to enlarge it. If you want to add the sender details to your address

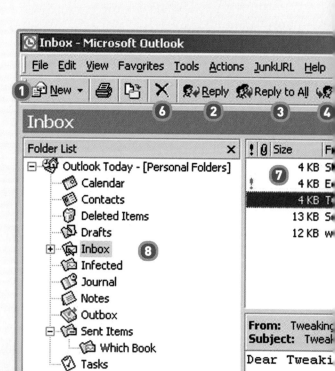

Warning!

Email is the most common way for viruses to spread. Be wary of opening messages with attachments unless you are (a) running an anti-virus package and (b) absolutely certain you know the sender and are expecting an attachment from him or her. Do not be fooled by apparently plausible messages or senders. Update your anti-virus software at least weekly.

book, select the Tools menu and select '**Add to Address Book**'. You are then presented with a form so that, if you wish, you can add extra details such as telephone number and postal address

10 The header toolbar allows you to organise your mailbox quickly, either by sender's name (from), the email's subject, the

date received or according to how the sender has described you. Click on the heading to sort by that column. Click on the heading again to sort the other way round (e.g. most recent first/oldest first)

11 Clicking on a link within an email launches your web browser and loads the indicated page

12 This box shows a preview of the email message that has been selected. Double-clicking on an email in window 7 will expand the view to full size.

Are you getting attached?

As well as containing text, emails can also have files attached to them. Emails with an attached file normally have a paper clip displayed to the left of the message. To save an attachment from an email on to your PC, open the email by double-clicking on it, then select '**File**', then select '**Save all attachments**'. The computer prompts you for a location in which to save the attached documents and the files are transferred to your PC.

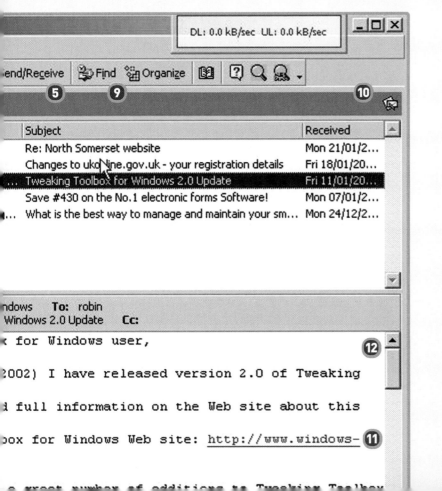

DOWNLOADING SOFTWARE

Downloading times

With a standard 56K modem connected to a fast website, downloading can be a slow process. A good rule of thumb is to allow five minutes for every 1Mb of data being downloaded. Heavy traffic on some websites may reduce the speed of downloading. To help users, some of the bigger sites offer alternative websites (called mirrors), which are located in different countries. A mirror site for a download with a .uk suffix may provide a much faster download than a US-based website.

If downloading is very slow, it may be worth connecting at a different time of day, when there is less congestion.

If you are fortunate to have ADSL or a cable modem with download speeds up to ten times faster than the best modem connection, you will find that downloads which should normally last for two or more hours will take less than 15 minutes.

The Internet is a source for tens of thousands of programs, music, pictures and documents which can be downloaded on to your computer. You can search for these by an engine such as google.com, altavista.com or yahoo.com.

In this example we are downloading a game from one of the world's largest online collections of shareware and freeware: www.cnet.shareware.com

This site has thousands of programs available for download. They include educational programs, financial software, games and utilities. The site also helps you search elsewhere on the Internet. The entry for this game details its author and size. Clicking on the **'Download now'** link starts the download process. A program of this size would take some time on a slow link.

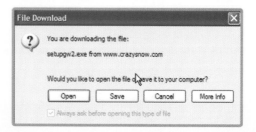

Before the file starts to download, Internet Explorer will ask you if you want to save it on your computer. If you choose **'Save'**, you are given the option of specifying where on your hard disk it is to be saved. The option **'Open'** is not advised. Saving the file to disk, regardless of its size, allows you to check it for viruses.

As the file downloads, you will receive a constant status report as to the speed of the download and, normally, how much time is required to finish the download.

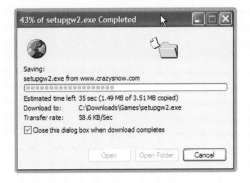

When the file has downloaded, you will receive confirmation of this and a new icon will appear in the folder in which you chose to save the file. Very often the file is stored in a compressed format known as a zipped file. This is uncompressed by a suitable utility, the most common of which is WinZip, a shareware program freely available on magazine-cover CD-ROMs or by download.

Once WinZip is installed, clicking on the zipped file you have just downloaded will begin the unzipping process.

After the unzipping process has finished, you will be left with a new folder containing the new program's files.

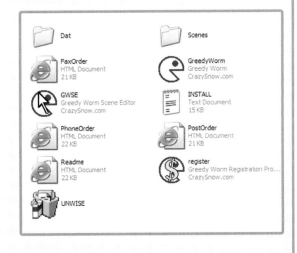

Shareware *vs* freeware

Shareware programs are often complete software applications that the authors have decided to make available for evaluation purposes in the hope that users who like the software will buy it at a future date. Although shareware is free, technical assistance and/or upgrades may be available only to users who have paid.

Freeware, on the other hand, consists of full programs, created by the authors for altruistic reasons. As such, no payment is expected.

Some freeware, such as RealPlayer, QuickTime and browsers like Internet Explorer and Netscape Navigator, are offered free with constant improvements and good technical support. The authors of freeware make money from other packages that complement the free products or through selling advertising or mailing lists generated from the free user base.

It is illegal to resell either shareware or freeware without the authors' consent.

INTERNET TROUBLESHOOTING

This section offers tips on how to solve some of the most common Internet problems, including unreliable or non-working connections and problems with email.

INTERNET BROWSER PROBLEMS

When I click on the Internet Explorer icon located on my desktop my connection doesn't automatically start.
Check in the File menu that 'Work offline' is not ticked. If you still do not connect, go to the Tools menu under Internet Explorer 6, select Internet Options/Connections and make sure that the box 'Always dial my default connection' is ticked. Earlier versions of Internet Explorer will have this option, but in a slightly different place in the Tools menu.

The Internet browser connects but the speed of my connection is very slow.
Every time you make a connection to your ISP, your modem tests line conditions during the call setup. If line conditions are poor, the transfer rate is reduced to improve reliability. Bad line conditions can be caused by heavy storms, lots of people making calls within your local area or a badly connected telephone extension box. Try reconnecting several times: you may get a better connection speed. Check the connection speed by clicking on the small green box that appears in the lower right-hand corner of the main desktop when a connection is made. The average for a 56K modem is between 40,000bps (40K) and 48,000bps (48K). Check in your modem settings that your maximum port speed is set at 115,200.

Some web pages fail to display correctly. Instead I get rubbish or error messages about 'scripting'.
Although having your security settings too high (see section 7.3) could cause this, it is more likely to be caused by having an old version of your browser. Internet Explorer version 5 and Netscape 4.79 upwards shouldn't cause problems. Netscape version 6 was somewhat problematic on release, but later upgrades have delivered a stable product. Windows XP comes with Internet Explorer version 6. Always check for updates of these products.

I type in my user name and password but the Internet browser fails to connect, giving me an incorrect password or login message instead.
Make sure that the Caps Lock key is not active when you type in the password or login as these are often case-sensitive.

If you get your password wrong too many times, some computer systems lock you out for a while. This is to prevent hackers trying common passwords from gaining entry to your ISP account. Wait 30 minutes and try again.

I get a connection to the Internet but this drops unexpectedly after a few minutes of use.
If you have other devices on the same phone line (e.g. fax or answerphone), try disconnecting them to see if reliability improves. Check the connections settings in Internet Explorer under Tools/Internet Options/ Connections/Settings/Advanced. The box saying **'Disconnect if idle for xx minutes'** should not be set for less than 5. Many do not tick this box at all.

EMAIL PROBLEMS

I am trying to send email to a friend but the mail never reaches the receiver. Instead I get either an error message or no indication of what went wrong.

If you are sending mail with a large attachment, it may have been blocked by the ISP because the attached file is too large. Try sending an email without an attachment to test this possibility.

Some ISPs block emails containing expletives or sexual terms. Check your ISP's policy on email content via its website or customer support service.

If using an address supplied by the address book, try typing in the email address manually as the address book may be corrupt or contain an incorrect entry.

I keep receiving junk email. Can I block this type of email?

To an extent. Some ISPs make an effort to block spam (as junk email is normally called). Hotmail makes a real effort to do this, but even so, lots gets through. The only certain way of avoiding spam is to not have an email address at all.

I've lost an important email among all my messages. How can I find it?

Like many applications, email packages often have a 'Find' utility. Within Outlook this is located under Edit/Find/Message. By typing in a word under the heading 'Message body' the software will locate and display any email containing the specified word.

I have received an email with an attachment that I cannot open.

Attached files from emails need a compatible application to be located on your system before it can read them. Make sure that the file is compatible with one of your applications, but instead of double-clicking on the attachment save it to your hard disk first using the 'Save Attachments' option available from the File menu of most email programs. Next, open the compatible application and load the file into it manually.

Email can be sent from many different types of computers including Apple Macintosh computers, UNIX-based systems and even hand-held computers. Some attachment types may not be compatible with PC architecture and therefore need to be converted before they can be used on a PC. Contact the sender to find out what type of computer and which application program created the attached file.

I want to check my home emails when I'm at work. Is this possible?

Often. Many ISPs offer web-based email for checking your email remotely. You will need your login name and password. Some web-based email services, such as Hotmail and Yahoo, allow you to check several POP3 email accounts as well as the web-based email account. Most home users use POP3 email accounts. This is especially helpful if your normal ISP does not have webmail.

Troubleshooting checklist

• If using an external modem, check whether the modem is plugged into the correct serial port on the computer. There may be more than one of these ports.

• Check whether the phone line is in use by another person or device.

• Check whether your ISP has changed its dial-in number.

• Check whether any fax software is running in the background. If so, turn it off and try again.

• Check that you have logged on under the correct user name.

• Check whether your ISP dial-up number is simply engaged due to heavy traffic.

• Check whether another phone on the same line is off the hook or waiting for a 'ring back' service.

SECURITY AND PRIVACY

This section offers tips on how to deal with one of the burning issues for many Internet users – how to protect your privacy and security. With the Internet growing in importance throughout the world in all areas of business, commerce and government, it is now essential for you to understand the implications of connecting your home PC to the Internet.

The dangers

Two threats exist. One is from viruses and the other from Trojans. Both are widespread and both can cause a great deal of trouble and nuisance to your PC.

How do viruses get on my PC?

There are two ways in which a virus can infect your PC. The most common way now is probably through Internet email. The second is by disk – normally a floppy disk, but occasionally a CD-ROM. It is quite common for infected floppy disks from other users' PCs to infect your computer.

How do I protect against viruses?

You need two ingredients. First, a good anti-virus package that is updated frequently. Second, a dose of common sense. Several anti-virus packages are available from PC retailers – both in the high street and via mail-order. Allowing for a degree of personal preference, your choice should be governed by the effectiveness of the software in detecting viruses. A good detection rate is key. If an anti-virus package does not detect every virus, what good is it? Several third-party companies test anti-virus software for detection rates. You can check out the latest statistics from ICSA (www.icsa.net), Virus Bulletin (www.virusbtn.com), West Coast Labs (www.check-mark.com), and HackFix (www.hackfix.org).

One key point to bear in mind: no anti-virus software is perfect. Most are pretty good but all are useless if you do not keep your package up-to-date. Remember that in a bad month, some 300–400 new viruses are released. One estimate suggests that a new virus is created every 18 seconds!

What are firewalls?

Firewalls are either hardware devices or software that protect computer systems from intrusion and attack by outsiders. Home users are unlikely to use a hardware device when good software is appropriate and available.

What is the cost?

For the home user, effective anti-virus software costs between £25 and £50. This will include free updates for one year, normally by downloading the update from the supplier's website. Some software is free, and a search on the Internet for free anti-virus software will reveal a few products, such as **AVG** and **Anti-vir**. All suppliers who charge for their products provide free evaluation copies and you will find one or more on most magazine CDs. AVG is developing a reputation for being good.

Common sense, of course, is free and should be applied when dealing with emails. Viruses are often spread by Outlook Express/Outlook address books becoming infected on a user's PC. It is now quite common for people to receive semi-plausible emails from unknown senders, or even from known people. These carry a 'payload' which attaches itself to the address book and spreads itself to all the people listed. The key here is to be ultra-cautious and not open any files attached to an email from an unknown, suspicious or untrustworthy source, or even from a known person if you are not expecting an attachment. All the major anti-virus vendors offer excellent advice about preventing infection. Read it and implement the suggestions. It is better to be safe than sorry.

Trojans

Trojans make viruses seem like harmless child's play. These programs will allow anyone on the Internet to control your computer remotely. Trojans let their creators collect all your passwords, access all your accounts including email, read and modify all your documents, publish the contents of your hard drive so it is shared across the Internet, record your keystrokes, look at your screen, and listen to your conversations on your computer's microphone – all without you ever knowing it is happening. If this sounds unlikely, go to http://grc.com/dos/ and read carefully – you will find that it is all completely true.

How do I protect against Trojans?

Basically you need to install some anti-Trojan software and a personal firewall. There are several packages which will protect against Trojans, including BOClean, Zone Alarm Pro, Tiny Personal Firewall and others. The last two of these are free.

Protecting your privacy

This is much more difficult and a topic most home users rarely consider, although interest is growing. If you surf the Net, you leave a trail. All sorts of tricks are used by website developers to collect information about their visitors – cookies being the most well known. The Internet has a number of sites which are devoted to the topic of privacy and ways of protecting it. Be warned, if you are determined to be anonymous, achieving your aim can involve using processes that can be tiresome and may require the purchase of special software. You may find it simpler never to connect to the Net in the first place! If this topic interests you, type 'Internet privacy' into your favourite search engine and explore the topic.

INTRODUCING NEWSGROUPS

And now the weather . . .

Unlike the rest of the Internet, newsgroups are rarely affected by Internet weather (busy times that slow down data transfer rates). Most big ISPs host newsgroups on a local server and, as such, accessing them is just a single hop from you to your ISP.

Few ISPs host all available newsgroups (some 85,000 and rising daily). Most in the UK exclude the more pornographic, racist and hateful. Some exclude newsgroups that others carry. Most ISPs will consider requests for non-contentious additions.

Newsgroups are similar to electronic notice-boards, often used as an area where like-minded people can get together and discuss ideas, solve problems or just voice their opinions. Newsgroups are unregulated and may therefore contain text and pictures that are unsuitable for children. Some ISPs restrict or censor newsgroups for this reason. Your ISP may also provide some newsgroups available only to subscribers to its services.

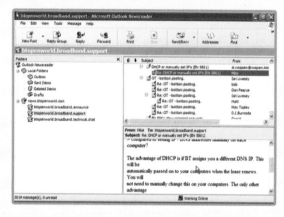

Getting started

Of the various newsgroup readers, many are free and some come as part of email programs. This example shows Microsoft Outlook Express, which is a particularly common newsreader. When you connect for the first time you need to supply some details, the most important of which is the name of the news server to which

you wish to attach. In most cases this will be called:
news.the_name_of_your_ISP.co.uk

You can also specify an email address and description of yourself so that other newsgroup users can reply to you directly.

If the newsreader requires any passwords or login names, you will need to contact your ISP for them.

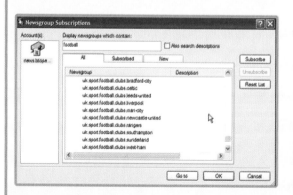

Searching for newsgroups

Once you are connected, the newsreader lists all the available newsgroups. This procedure can take quite a while as some servers have over 50,000 groups listed, on subjects

Typical newsreader software

1 Post a new message in this newsgroup

2 Replies can be sent either to the author or the whole newsgroup

3 Allows you to search for a specific newsgroup or just browse any that appeal to you

4 **Message display**: a small '+' next to one indicates that there are several responses from others. Clicking on the '+' displays the responses

5 Preview of the message you have selected. Messages can have attached documents. In this

package, an attached document is indicated by a paper clip in the top right-hand portion of the preview window. To save an attachment, use the File/Save As option on the menu bar

6 List of all the newsgroups to which you currently subscribe

Warning!

Newsgroups are notorious for viruses, pornography and foul language. To avoid such groups, look for ones described as 'moderated', but be aware that although this means that someone with the power to remove undesirable messages is watching this newsgroup, there is no guarantee that the moderator has the same value system as you.

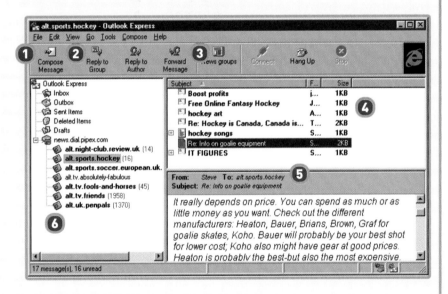

ranging from cookery to Japanese politics.

Newsgroup names follow a format similar to Internet website names: e.g. alt.food.cooking.French is part of the ALTernative server under the folder Food, under the subfolder

Cooking under the subfolder French.

From this interface you can also do a search for newsgroups which contain a word that you have specified.

If you click on a group and select '**Subscribe**', the name will be added to your

newsgroup list for convenient selection in the future.

If you select '**Go to**', the software will attempt to download the headers in that group and then display them with just the header information.

CREATING YOUR OWN WEBSITE

Free – or almost

Most free space offers from ISPs come with a catch. In many cases you will have to take advertisement banners on your site or be prepared to sell your non-confidential user details to advertisers. Many of these websites also have a limit on the number of Mb your site may contain. And if you need technical help, you may find you're out of luck.

Creating a website is all the rage. Whether for business or pleasure, website design is akin to desktop publishing (DTP). Like DTP software, many web-design programs use a simple cut-and-paste interface to lay out text and graphics. Most of the tools are free and many ISPs are providing web space at very low cost. This section looks at the four main steps for creating a website.

STEP 1 Get some space for your website from an Internet service provider (ISP)

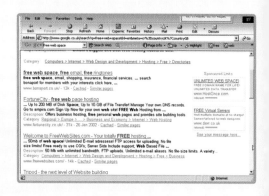

Most ISPs now offer space on their servers for users to host their own websites. Try doing a search on your ISP's home page, using phrases such as **'free web space'** or **'hosting a web page'**. If your ISP does not offer this service or it is expensive, try one of the many websites that offer free hosting. In most cases you simply supply some details about yourself and choose a web address. For free sites, the suffix of the address will normally be that of the host, e.g. myhomepage@freeisp.co.uk.

Once you have signed up, you need a web-creation program.

STEP 2 Design your web pages

A website is a bit like a tree, with a trunk from which sprout branches and leaves. The first page is called the **'home page'**, from which you can link to other pages, which can carry further links, and so on.

Every website is created using HyperText Mark-up Language (HTML). To create a layered structure similar to the one on the right you can use software like that used for DTP, such as Microsoft Frontpage, Adobe PageMill and Dreamweaver, which allows you to lay out text and graphics and create links to other pages. Many software packages for creating websites are available free. To find one, go to a popular shareware

STEP 3 Upload your site from your local PC to your ISP's web server

Your website-creation software allows you to look at your website while running on your PC. Once you are satisfied with the results, you need to upload to the web server that will be hosting your website. To do this, you need a file transfer protocol (FTP) program: CuteFTP is one of the most popular FTP software packages and is suitable for the beginner.

Before you can begin the upload, your FTP software needs to be set up with the address of the ISP hosting your website, your user name and password and possibly the name of the folder to which the files are going to be transferred. This information will be supplied to you by your ISP.

The FTP program then connects to the Internet and attempts to upload any file you tell it to. Simply select the folder containing your website from your local hard disk and send it to your Internet web space.

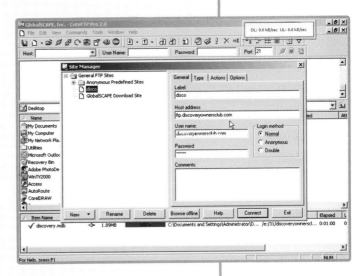

STEP 4 Improving your website

Once you have uploaded your website, you may have to wait a few hours while the ISP and the rest of the Internet recognise it. Once it is up, you can alter it simply by changing the index page to add more links for new pages and/or change graphics by redesigning the pages and uploading any changed files to the website, making sure you use the same name as the old page. To add some spice to your website you can add animations, sound, even links to other people's sites. If you want your own special web address – e.g. www.robinshomepage.co.uk – you can get these from as little as £5 for two years. You do not have to change your website: you just point this address to your website.

You can also register with the search engines – this is free in most cases – by specifying a description of your site or by the search engine taking text from your site's first page and adding this into its database. If someone types into a search engine something that matches your site, it may display it on the search results page. The more unique a group of words you have, the better the chance of a successful search.

Internet site such as download.com or use a search engine like Google, Yahoo or Altavista. Then type in a phrase such as **'web page design'** or **'HTML editor'**. Whichever you choose, do not be afraid to experiment and do use the help system's instructions on how to use your chosen package.

Remember:
• make sure your first page is called 'Index'
• put all your individual pages and images in the same folder for ease of reference
• try to use compressed graphic files such as JPEG or GIF for pictures to reduce loading time for visitors.

A

ActiveX Software that enables Multimedia content from the Internet to be directly embedded in the Windows operating system

ADSL (asymmetrical digital subscriber line) is a technology for transmitting digital information at a high bandwidth on existing phone lines. ADSL is an 'always on' connection and for home users downloads at 512Kb. ADSL is asymmetric in that it uses most of the channel to transmit downstream to the user and only a small part to receive information from the user. It simultaneously accommodates analogue (voice) information on the same line

AGP (accelerated graphics port) An interface (q.v.) that enables your PC to use especially high-performance 3D graphics cards capable of displaying particularly complex images, notably in games

analogue/analog Means of electronic transmission. Analogue signals are continuous and can vary infinitesimally. A good example is the human voice, which is why telephone and broadcast communications were designed to use analogue technology. Early computers were analogue but all current PCs are digital (q.v.). A modem converts a signal from digital to analogue or *vice versa*, to enable digital computers to use analogue telephone lines

anti-virus software A special program designed to intercept viruses (destructive programs, q.v.) on your PC and stop them from causing harm, or fix damage caused by viruses

API (application programming interface) A gateway or link within a program that allows other software to interact with it

applet A small program, especially one written in Java (q.v.) and downloaded from the Internet

application/application program Software that performs a specific function directly for the user or, in some cases, for another application program. Examples of applications include word processors, database programs, spreadsheets, web browsers, drawing, painting and image editing

Athlon A high-performance PC processor launched in 1999 by AMD as a competitor to Intel's market-leading Pentium III (q.v.) chip

attachment A file that is specially encoded and sent with an email (q.v.) message. An attachment, typically, is a file saved using a particular application (e.g. a word-processing program), so the recipient of the attachment must have an application capable of opening the file. This way of sending information preserves the format of the file – e.g. for a text document, the tabs, font sizes, etc.

AVI (audio video interleaved) A highly compressed sound and motion picture file for playback on a PC with suitable software. AVI players include Realvideo, RealPlayer, Microsoft Mediaplayer and Apple Quicktime. AVI files have the suffix .avi

B

backup A copy of a computer file made in case anything happens to the original. Backups can be made on hard disks, floppy disks, CD-ROMs, cartridges, computer tapes: in fact, on anything which allows you to have a second distinct copy

binary The base-two number system that computers use to represent digital data. '0' and '1' are the only binary digits; 2 in decimal (the base-ten number system) is represented as 10 in binary. The great advantage of a digital (q.v.) binary system is that the only possible values are simply the presence of a pulse (meaning 1) or its absence (meaning 0). The size of the pulse is not important

BIOS (basic input-output system) The BIOS stores fundamental information about the PC setup (amount of memory, hard-disk size, etc.) and controls the PC when it starts up

bit The smallest unit of data used by a PC. Eight bits combine to make a byte, which is roughly one character of text

Bluetooth A new wireless standard for connecting electronic devices. Examples of appliances that use this technology are hands-free kits for mobile phones and digital cameras able to send pictures to desktop PCs

bookmark To record the address of an Internet site (because you may wish to return to it later). Bookmarking a site saves time because you have no need to key in its address

boot-up The start-up procedure for a PC. Controlled by the BIOS (q.v.), it starts the computer, finds an operating system (OS, q.v.), then passes on basic information about the system to the OS

bps (bits per second) A common measure of speed for data communications. The speed of transmission via a modem (q.v.) is often measured in this way

browser A program used for navigating the Worldwide Web. The two most common browsers are Microsoft Internet Explorer and Netscape Navigator

bubblejet printer *See* inkjet printer

bug A coding error in a computer program which may cause the program to behave erratically

button A small panel on the screen image showing words such as 'OK' or 'Cancel'. Press on the button (with the mouse) to make your choice

byte Comprising eight bits (q.v.) of computer data, a byte is roughly equivalent to one character of text

C

cabinet (CAB) file A single computer file created to hold a number of compressed files. A set of cabinet files can be contained in a folder. During the installation of a program, the compressed files in a cabinet are decompressed and copied to an appropriate directory for the user. Cabinet files are similar to the ZIP file standard. A cabinet file usually carries the suffix .cab

cache A storage device for frequently used information which reduces the time an application takes to access information. For instance, a web browser stores pages visited on your disk, so that if you visit them again it has only to check for changes, as most of the information is already in your computer. RAM cache is extra-fast memory for storing data until the processor needs it

CAD (computer-aided design) Special software used by architects, engineers, draughtsmen, artists and others to create precision drawings and technical illustrations. CAD software can be used to create two-dimensional (2D) drawings or three-dimensional (3D) models

CD-ROM Compact disk read-only memory: a CD, of the same size and shape as an audio CD, that can hold about 700Mb of computer data (text, pictures, movies etc.). CD-ROMs are read in a special CD-ROM drive which can also play music CDs but cannot write to any CDs. CD drives are being superseded by DVD (q.v.) drives, which use disks that can store much higher volumes

CD writer A special type of CD-ROM drive which allows you to write to blank CDs. The two types of disks are CD-Rs, which are written to once, and CD-RWs, which are written to over and over again

Celeron A budget range of PC processors from Intel (q.v.)

chip A tiny piece of semiconductor material, such as silicon, processed for use in an integrated circuit or component

chipset The chips used on the motherboard of a PC to allow the processor to talk to other PC components such as the memory and hard disk

client A requesting program or user in a client/server system – e.g. the user of a web browser (q.v.), who makes requests, as a client, for pages from servers on the Internet. The browser itself is a client in the context of its relationship with the computer from which it is getting information

clip art Ready-made drawings or illustrations, arranged by category, that can be freely copied by cutting and pasting into your own documents. Clip art often comes free with applications which can use it (such as word-processing and presentation software), but themed packages are also available

clock speed The speed at which a PC processor can deal with instructions – e.g. a clock speed of 700MHz means that the chip can handle 700 million sets of instructions every second

codec (coder/decoder or compression/decompression) Used to describe software, integrated circuits, or chips that perform data conversion. In this context, the term is an acronym for 'coder/decoder'. This type of codec combines analogue-to-digital conversion and digital-to-analogue conversion functions in a single chip or via a software application

COM1, COM2, COM3 The common names for the PC's serial connections, used for modems, printers, etc. *See* serial communication

compression Reduction of the space taken up by a file by encoding the data in it more efficiently

Control Panel The command centre for Windows and other operating systems. You can use it to set and access options for your printer, soundcard, graphics card and much more

cookie Information stored on your hard disk by a website. It may include a user name and your own preferences, so that the next time you visit it is customised for you

copy A command which lets you copy information from one document to another (which may be controlled by the same or a different application)

CPU (central processing unit) Also called processor (q.v.) or microprocessor. The principal chip inside a PC, which provides most of its power and directs how all its functions are carried out

crash Malfunction of a program or the PC itself signalled by the screen freezing. The cause may be trivial and the easiest cure may be to restart the PC

CRT (cathode-ray tube) The core of a monitor, this is a vacuum-filled cone with a phosphor coating on the inside of the screen. Controlled by the PC's graphics card, an electron gun fires electrons at the screen, where they make the phosphor glow to create the image. Flat screens, used in laptop computers, use different technology and not CRTs

cut A command which lets you move a selected section of a document to a clipboard from which you can paste it into another document

D

DAT (digital audio tape) A standard medium for the digital recording (of professional quality) of sound on tape. A DAT drive is a digital tape-recorder which can record at sample rates of up to 48KHz, greater even than the CD audio standard. Digital inputs and outputs on professional DAT decks allow the user to transfer recordings from the DAT tape to an audio workstation for precise editing. The compact size and low cost of the DAT medium makes it an excellent way to compile recordings that are going to be used to create a CD master

database A program for storing information on a PC in a structured format which enables you to determine the relationships between different items of data as well as offering powerful search capabilities. A simple database is like a card-index file which can be viewed by any item in any order

defrag/defragmentation The process of cleaning up a hard disk by shuffling all the contents of the disk so that each file is stored neatly in one area and all the empty space is together too. This speeds up data retrieval. *See also* fragmentation

desktop The first Windows screen you see when your PC has finished running through the start-up routine. Made to resemble a real desktop, it displays icons (q.v.) that provide shortcuts to programs and data files

dialogue/dialog box A message window, displayed by Windows or by a program, and demanding some sort of response from the user

digital Means of electronic transmission via signals that comprise separate pulses, each of which can take only one of a set of specific values. Early computers used the alternative analogue (q.v.) technology. Digital computers proved much more reliable; hence, all current PCs are digital

digital camera A camera which records photos in memory rather than on film, so you can download pictures straight to your PC. It uses a light-sensitive panel to convert images into a computer file

DIMM (dual in-line memory module) A module containing several RAM (q.v.) chips on a small circuit board with pins that connect it to the computer's motherboard (q.v.). A DIMM has a 168-pin connector and supports 64-bit data transfer. DIMM is by far the most common type of computer memory

directory Also known as a folder, this is a structure or area for keeping files together on a disk. Folders can be nested inside other folders, which are themselves inside other folders

DirectX Developed by Microsoft, DirectX is a range of multimedia add-ons for Windows. It allows games developers and hardware designers to ensure that all their products work together

DOS (disk operating system) A basic PC operating system (q.v.) that uses typed commands rather than the graphics of Windows. Early versions of Windows are based on DOS

dot-matrix printer Machine which makes up text and images from dots created by striking tiny pins against an inked ribbon, much like a typewriter. Now largely superseded by inkjet and laser printers but sometimes used with carbon-copy forms, e.g. for multi-part invoice printing

download To transfer files or data to a PC, either from the Internet or from another device such as a digital camera

dpi (dots per inch) A measure of the sharpness (i.e. the density of illuminated points) on a display screen or printer. The dpi for a given screen resolution varies according to the overall size of the screen

drag and drop A way of moving a highlighted file or selected part of a document by clicking and holding the mouse button, then dragging the selection to a new location and dropping it by releasing the button

driver A small program needed for making a specific computer accessory, such as a printer, work properly with a PC

DTP (desktop publishing) The design and layout of magazines, books and other documents using a computer. DTP software gives the user great control over layout and flexibility in printing

Duron A range of budget processors made by AMD

DVD (digital versatile disk) A DVD looks like a CD but uses a different type of laser with improved media and can hold up to 17Gb of data — more than enough for a full-length movie. A DVD drive can play CDs but a CD drive cannot use DVDs

E

email (electronic mail) A means of sending messages and file attachments from one computer to another across the Internet or a local network

ethernet A standard for linking computers together to form a local network, generally in an office environment

execute (executable and .EXE files) To execute a program is to run it on a computer. In Windows 98, program file names normally include the suffix .EXE

expansion card A small circuit board that can be plugged into the motherboard (q.v.) of a computer to add more functions to it. Examples include modems, network cards and soundcards

expansion slot The electrical connector on the motherboard (q.v.) into which an expansion card is plugged

extension Suffix: the three letters after the dot in a PC filename; typically, they indicate the type or format of the file

F

FAQ (frequently asked question) A common abbreviation, used on websites, newsgroups, etc. to describe a page or a file which tries to answer the most common – and obvious – questions about the site. This saves you time as you can find the answers quickly, and also saves the website staff or newsgroup regulars from answering the same questions over and over again

favorite The name given by Internet Explorer (q.v.) for an Internet site you visit often — 'bookmarked' (q.v.) — so you can jump to it from a list rather than having to type in its address every time

file extension See extension

FireWire A super-fast data link between the PC and external devices. The generic term for this technology is the IEEE1394 standard

flatbed scanner A scanner that looks like the top half of a photocopier. The document (text or picture) is placed face-down on a sheet of glass for scanning and is then stored as a file on the PC

floppy disk A small removable disk holding up to 1.44Mb of data which can be used for storing files or for transferring them from one PC to another

font A particular design or style of typeface, e.g. Times, Helvetica, Univers

format To prepare a completely blank disk so that the operating system can write information to it. Essentially, it provides an address for each physical part of the disk so that the PC can find the information again

fragmentation A new hard disk writes each new file to a virgin area. As files are amended (being increased or reduced in size, re-saved or deleted), the stored data gets dispersed to different locations on the disk (fragmented), the various items of data being reunited when you retrieve the file. This process of joining the data together again slows down the PC; defragmentation (q.v.) cleans up the disk and improves performance by moving the segments of files back together

FTP (file transfer protocol) A method of transferring files from one computer to another across the Internet. FTP is commonly used to download large files or to load documents into a website

G

Gb (gigabyte) A measurement of storage space equal to 1,024Mb

GIF (graphics interchange format) A type of graphics file commonly used to display images on the Internet

graphics card The part of a PC that controls what is displayed on screen

GUI (graphical user interface) A method of driving software by means of windows, menus, buttons, icons and so on. For example, while DOS (q.v.) uses only text, Windows — a GUI system — uses pictures to show you what is happening on the screen

H

hacking A slang term for gaining unauthorised access to other people's computer systems and networks, or for making unauthorised changes to software programs

hard disk A magnetic storage device capable of holding huge amounts of data. It is used in a PC to hold Windows, programs and users' files

hardware The computer and its peripherals (q.v.): the tangible part of a computer's set-up. Programs are known as software

homepage The first, introductory page seen by visitors to a website

HTML (hypertext mark-up language) A coded language used to describe how a web page should look. When the page is loaded into a browser such as Netscape Navigator or Internet Explorer (q.v.), the browser interprets the HTML and displays the page correctly

hyperlink A clickable link (usually underlined) which lets you jump between websites, documents, or places in a document

I

icon A tiny symbol displayed on screen to represent an application, file or command

IDE (integrated drive electronics) The most common standard for connecting hard disks, CD-ROM drives etc. in a PC. Alternatives include the faster, but more expensive, SCSI (q.v.)

image editing The process of manipulating or altering photos or illustrations on a PC, using applications such as PhotoShop, PaintShop Pro or Corel Draw

infrared port A means of connecting a PC to other devices and computers, transmitting data using infrared light rather than using wires; similar to the port on a television that receives instructions from the remote control buttons

inkjet printer One that squirts precisely controlled droplets of ink on to the paper to build up the image. Although they are relatively cheap, modern inkjet printers can produce pictures that are almost indistinguishable from photographs. However, they are slow and the ink these printers use is expensive. Some manufacturers use the term 'bubblejet' instead of 'inkjet'

Intel Maker of the 8086, 80286 and Pentium ranges of processors which are used in IBM PCs and compatible computers

interface Design feature that allows different electronic devices to communicate with each other. Programs interact with their users by means of a 'user interface', defined by its 'look and feel' and overall design. The standards by which peripherals and PC components communicate with the computer itself are also known as interfaces

Internet International network of computers. Developed from US military and academic networks, the Internet is now easily accessible from most computers on company networks or computers connected to telephone lines via modems

Internet Explorer Microsoft's browser, included with all versions of Windows

Interrupt ReQuest (IRQ) An assigned location where the computer can expect a device to interrupt it when the device sends the computer signals about its operation. For example, when a printer has finished printing, it sends an interrupt signal to the computer. The signal momentarily interrupts the computer so that it can decide what processing to do next. Since multiple signals to the computer on the same interrupt line might not be understood by the computer, a unique value must be specified for each device and its path to the computer. Devices can share IRQ, although this can sometimes cause an error or a conflict

intranet Internal computer network used within an organisation

IRC (Internet relay chat) A means of 'chatting' to other Internet users using real-time typed messages

ISA (industry standard architecture) A slot design found in older PCs for attaching expansion cards so that devices such as a screen or soundcard can be added to the system. Modern PCs are more likely to use a newer slot design, PCI (q.v.)

ISDN (integrated services digital network) A digital telephone line that allows you to send and receive data more quickly than a normal telephone connection. It is used for high-volume direct data transfer and for Internet access

ISP (Internet service provider) Although it is possible to connect a computer directly to the Internet, this is too expensive for most companies and home users. Instead, an ISP connects its computers to the Internet and then allows its customers (both corporate and domestic) to connect to these, thus linking to the Net indirectly

J

Java A special programming language used chiefly on websites to add sophisticated animations and interactive effects

joystick A device that lets you control movement, especially in computer games

JPEG (joint picture experts group) A type of graphics file, commonly used to display images on the Internet or for presentations. It can be very highly compressed so that the pictures take up less space

jumpers These connect the little metal pins found on expansion cards (q.v.) and PC motherboards (q.v.), allowing you to change settings manually

K

K56flex An early 56Kbits/sec modem technology. If your modem is a K56flex model, ensure that it can be upgraded to the modern V90 standard

K6, K6-2, K6-III PC processors made by AMD (American Micro Devices), a major rival to Intel in the CPU market

Kb (kilobyte) A unit of data, equal to 1,024 bytes (q.v.). This is enough to store just over 1,000 characters of text

Kbits/sec (kilobits per second; Kbps) A measure of data transfer speed, often used to compare modem specifications (8Kbits = 1Kb)

L

LAN (local area network) Network of computers that are physically near each other, e.g. in the same office

laptop computer Small (telephone-directory-size) portable computer that can be used away from a power source. Laptops are much more expensive than desktop computers

laser printer A type of printer which uses a laser beam to generate high-quality text and graphics. Black and white laser printers are generally affordable but colour models remain expensive

li-ion (lithium ion) The most sophisticated type of rechargeable battery, used in many notebook computers (q.v.). It is light and offers very high power capacity, but is expensive

Linux (often pronounced LIH-nuhks with a short 'i') is a UNIX-like operating system that was designed to provide personal computer users with a free or very low-cost operating system comparable to traditional and usually more expensive UNIX or Windows systems

login The process of connecting a computer to a network or to an ISP (q.v.). The user name you enter in order to identify yourself is also called a login

LPT1, LPT2 The DOS names (from 'line printer') for the PC's parallel connections, used for printers, scanners and disk drives. *See* parallel communication

LS-120 A type of disk drive that can store 120Mb of data on a single disk of the same size as a floppy disk. The drives can also read and write to normal floppies

M

Macintosh (popularly, 'Mac') Introduced in 1984 by Apple Computers, this was the first widely sold personal computer with a graphical user interface (GUI) (q.v.)

Mb (megabyte) A measure of computer processor storage and real and virtual memory; one Mb is 1,048,576 bytes (q.v.)

Mbps (millions of bits per second, or **megabits per second)** A measure of band width, or data-carrying capacity, representing the total information flow over a second: hence, speed of transmission of data, between computers, between computer and printer, around the Internet, and so on

microprocessor *See* processor

modem (modulator/demodulator) A device that modulates ingoing and outgoing signals from a computer or other digital device for transmission over conventional copper twisted pair telephone lines. It superimposes a digital (q.v.) data signal over a carrier to enable the computer data to travel over an analogue (q.v.) telephone line, and the modem at the other end extracts the data from the carrier so that it can travel digitally again

monitor The piece of computer equipment that provides the screen

motherboard The physical base that contains the computer's basic circuitry and components. Common components on a motherboard include CPU, RAM and ISA/PCI interface sockets (q.v.)

MPEG (moving picture experts group)
A standard for digital video and digital audio compression. The most common standards for video are MPEG Video and MP3 Audio

MP3 (MPEG-1 audio layer-3) A standard technology and format for compressing a sound sequence into a very small file while preserving the original level of sound quality

multimedia Combined use of media (e.g. sound, graphics, video, text)

N

Net See Internet

Netscape Web browser, available as Navigator or the more recent Communicator, and the company that developed it

NetWare A provider of software and protocols for networking between servers and clients' PCs; part of the Novell Corporation

network Group of computers linked together so that they can share files and resources such as printers and Internet access

newsgroups International discussion areas on the Internet, covering a huge range of topics

notebook computer Similar to, but slightly smaller than, a laptop computer (q.v.)

O

OpenGL (open graphics library)
The computer industry's standard application program interface (API) for defining 2D and 3D graphic images

operating system The software that controls the computer and provides basic functions for applications (e.g. allows a word processor to open and save files). Microsoft Windows is the most commonly used operating system

P

parallel communication One of two traditional standards (the other being serial, q.v.) for transmitting data. *See* LPT1, LPT2

PCI (peripheral component interconnect)
A slot design for connecting expansion cards to a PC

PCMCIA (Personal Computer Memory Card International Association)
Sometimes called PC card, this is a standard for a credit-card-sized memory or input-output device that fits into a notebook or laptop computer

PDA (personal digital assistant)
A small, hand-held device that provides computing facilities, and information storage and retrieval for personal or business users, usually for keeping track of schedules and addresses

Pentium The Pentium is the most common processor (q.v.) for computers. First produced by Intel in 1993, it has developed through the Pentium II, Pentium III and now the Pentium IV version

peripherals Hardware items separate from the PC, such as printers, screens (monitors) and scanners

PGP (pretty good privacy) A system for securing documents by means of encryption

pixel Derived from 'picture element', this is the basic unit of programmable colour on a computer display or in a computer image

plug and play *See* PnP

PnP (plug and play) A technology that gives computer users the ability to plug a device into a computer and have the computer recognise it automatically

port Socket

PowerPC A microprocessor architecture developed jointly by Apple, IBM and Motorola used in Apple Macintosh computers and some IBM computers

processor/microprocessor The 'engine' of any PC: the silicon chip that does all the work, e.g. Pentium, PowerPC. *See also* CPU

program *See* application

protocol A special set of rules for communicating between computer systems

Q

QWERTY A keyboard with a top row of letter keys starting Q,W,E,R,T,Y

R

registry (Windows Registry, Internet Registry) In the Microsoft Windows operating systems, the registry is a single location for keeping such information as devices attached, system options and what application programs are to be loaded when the operating system is stored

Registered Jacks (RJ-11, RJ-14, RJ-45) A series of telephone connection interfaces registered with the United States Federal Communications Commission. The USA, Europe and Asia all have different jack types. RJ-45 plugs and sockets are generally used in ethernet networks (q.v.)

RAM (random access memory) Memory that can be read from and written to; usually expressed in megabytes (q.v.), e.g. 8Mb

reset To restart the PC either by pressing the reset button or using the Ctrl+Alt+Del combination of keys. Also known as a 'warm boot', as the power is not turned off. A reset is often used after a system crash (q.v.), but only if normal restart methods are unsuccessful, as resetting can lead to the loss of unsaved data or corrupt files

ROM (read-only memory) Storage device that holds data permanently and may not be changed by the programmer

S

screen saver Moving graphic which appears on the monitor after a set period of time; open applications are still active. If a CRT-based monitor is left with the same image displayed for a long time, the image begins to burn in (so that you still see that image when the screen is turned off). To stop this happening, screen savers always have moving pictures

scroll bar Strip that appears along the right side and/or bottom of a window when the document contains more than can be displayed in the window, with arrows allowing you to 'scroll' up, down or across the document

SCSI (small computer system interface) Developed at Apple Computers, this is a set of standard electronic interfaces that allow personal computers to communicate with peripheral hardware such as disk drives, tape drives, CD-ROM drives, printers and scanners faster and more flexibly than previous interfaces. Not all PCs use this. *See also* IDE

search engine Means of searching the Internet, e.g. Yahoo, Lycos, Altavista, Google

sector Defined portion of a disk

serial communication One of two traditional standards (the other being parallel) for transmitting data. *See* COM1, COM2

server In a network (q.v.) of computers, the computer that has the main hard disk or storage for the other machines. In some networks, the server will also run applications for clients attached to it, passing information to the client on request

shareware Software that is distributed free on a trial basis in the hope that the user may want to buy it later

shortcut key Key combination that allows you to carry out a particular command quickly, e.g. Ctrl+Esc brings up the task list (q.v.)

software Series of programs that tell the computer what to do, e.g. WordPerfect and Word for word processing, Excel for spreadsheets

spreadsheet Application used for arithmetical calculations such as budgets, costings and quotations

status bar A display at the bottom of a window that shows information about a process, function or selected item

subdirectory (or folder) A subdivision of the files on a disk

T

task list A pop-up menu displaying all of the currently running applications

TCP/IP (transmission control protocol/Internet protocol) The standard used by every PC to enable it to move information around the Internet, so that NetWare, Unix, Windows and Apple computers can all communicate with each other. The network control panel includes TCP/IP settings which may prevent Internet access unless they are set correctly

Telnet An Internet service, used for computer games involving many participants, that allows you to log on to a computer somewhere else via the Internet and use it as if you were sitting in front of it

title bar Part of a window or dialog box that shows the name of either the application running in the window or the dialog box. The title bar in the currently selected window is a different colour from those for inactive windows

toggle Item that can be selected or deselected with the same action

U

UNIX Computer operating system (q.v.) designed to be used by many people at the same time (as in companies, organisations, universities or groups maintained by ISPs)

upload To transfer files from your PC to another (opposite of download, q.v.)

URL (uniform resource locator) The address of a web page

USB (universal serial bus) Standard for transmitting data that is faster than traditional serial or parallel communication. All modern PCs incorporate USB sockets so that expansion cards are not necessary. Devices connected by USB can be added or removed without the need to turn the PC off (i.e. hot-swapping)

utility Tool for making a specific task easier (e.g. mail-merge or email software) or for fixing problems

V

version Updated and 'improved' edition of a software package, often denoted by a higher number

VGA (video graphics adapter) This has come to mean the standard 15-pin socket used to connect a screen (monitor) to the computer

virus Destructive program specially designed to 'infect' and usually damage other applications. It can alter and delete data and cause serious computer system malfunctions

W

wallpaper Graphic image, the colour and pattern of which can be varied, displayed on desktop background. As documents are created, the wallpaper disappears until the user returns to the desktop

WAP (wireless application protocol) Standard for transmitting data between mobile phones and special Internet sites

warm boot *See* reset

Glossary

website Set of themed pages on the Worldwide Web (q.v.)

window Framed area on the screen in which you run applications and perform tasks. A window can be opened, closed, resized and moved

Windows (Microsoft Windows) Picture-based software which uses pull-down menus, dialog boxes and mouse-oriented operation. It was designed to make IBM PCs more user-friendly

word processing Application (q.v.) for handling text, allowing corrections to be made, and font/type size to be changed, spelling to be checked and words counted before the document is printed out

work station Single-user microcomputer; or, in a LAN, a PC that serves a single user

Worldwide Web (WWW) International network of computers which provides information and services in the form of websites (q.v.). Most small users who want their own website use a professional host (an ISP, q.v.) so that their site is available all the time

Z

ZIP A file extension (q.v.) for files compressed by the program PKZIP. Also a brand name for a popular type of removable disk

NUMERIC TERMS

286, 386, 486 Types of PC processor developed by Intel (q.v.) used in PCs before the Pentium chip (q.v.) was introduced. PCs using these chips are now outdated

3D graphics Images which appear to have depth and are much more realistic than flat (two-dimensional) ones; they demand a powerful PC and graphics card. 3D graphics are used in games and multimedia software, as well as in professional design packages

56Kbits/sec The current fastest speed for an analogue modem (q.v.) is shown theoretically as 56Kbits/sec, meaning that 56 kilobits of data per second can be sent down a phone line. In practice, however, the speed is more like 44Kbits/sec

Over 2,000 recognised file types are currently used by PC systems. In addition there are a number of file formats of programs which are no longer produced. The Internet has many places to download information stored as files. If you download a file which will not open via your favourite application, use this chart to find out what the file does and what application created it.

A

ABK Corel Draw AutoBackup
ABR Brush file (Adobe PhotoShop)
ABS MPEG Audio Sound file
ACAD Database file (AutoCAD)
ACB ACBM Graphic image
ACE Archiver Compression file
ACF Adobe custom filter (Adobe PhotoShop)
ACL Corel Draw 6 keyboard accelerator file
ACM Windows system directory file
ACO Colour Palette (Adobe PhotoShop)
ADF Amiga disk file
ADI AutoCAD device-independent binary plotter file
AFP Graphics file (IBM)
AIF Audio Interchange File for Macintosh applications
AMF Music file (Advanced Module Format)
ANI Microsoft Windows Animated cursor
ANS ANSI Text file
ART Clip Art
ASC ASCII Text file
ASF Microsoft Advanced Streaming Format
ASP Active Server Page
ASX Video file
ATM Adobe Type Manager data/info file
AU Audio U-law (pronounced mu-law)
AVI Microsoft Audio Video Interleaved file
AWD FaxView Document image

B

BAT Batch file
BDB Microsoft Works Dababase file
BFC Windows 95 Briefcase Document
BKS Microsoft Works Spreadsheet Backup
BMP Windows or OS/2 bitmap

C

CDA CD Audio Track
CDB Clipboard file
CHK File fragments saved by scan /defrag
COM Command file (program)
CPD Fax cover document

D

DAT Data file
DBW Microsoft Windows 9.x Database file
DCS Bitmap Graphics (Quark XPress)
DDB Bitmap Graphics file
DIB Device-independent bitmap
DIC Dictionary file
DOC WordStar document
DOC WordPerfect document
DOC Microsoft Word document
DOC DisplayWrite document
DOS Text file (DOS)
DOT Word Document Template (Microsoft Word for Windows)
DRV Device Driver (required to make a device function)

E

EML Microsoft Outlook Express mail message (MIME RFC 822)
EPS Encapsulated Postscript Vector graphics (Adobe Illustrator)
EPS Encapsulated PostScript image file
EPS Printer font (Epson, Xerox, Ventura Publisher)
EPSF Encapsulated PostScript
EXE Executable file

F

FAQ Frequently Asked Questions document
FAX Type image
FLI FLIC animation (AutoDesk)
FP3 FileMaker Pro database

G

GIF Bitmap (CompuServe)
GSM Audio stream Raw GSM (6.10 audio stream)

H

HLP Help file (Generic)
HTM A Web page (Hypertext Markup Language)

HTML A Web page (Hypertext Markup Language)

I

ICC Printer file (Kodak)
ICM Image Color Matching profile
ICO Icon (Microsoft Windows 3.x)
INF Install script (generic)
INI Initialisation file (generic)

J

JFF JPEG Image
JIF JPEG Image
JFIF JPEG Image
JPE JPEG Image
JPEG Compressed bitmap
JPG JPEG Bitmap

K

KEY Security file (such as a software registration number)
KYB Keyboard mapping (FTP)

L

LHA Compressed Archive (LHA/LHARC)
LWP Wordpro 96/97 file (Lotus)
LZH Compressed archive (LH ARC)

M

MDB Database (Microsoft Access)
MDL Model file (Quake)
MMF Mail message file (Microsoft Mail)
MME A multipart file in the Multi-Purpose Internet Mail Extensions (MIME) format
MOV Movie (QuickTime for Microsoft Windows)
MOV Movie (AutoCAD/AutoFlix)
MP2 MPEG Audio Layer 2
MP3 MPEG Audio Layer 3 (AC3)
MPEG Animation
MPG MPEG Animation
MSP Paint bitmap (Microsoft)

N

NSF Database (Lotus Notes)
NWS News message (Microsoft Outlook Express)

O

123 Lotus 1-2-3, '97 data file
ORG Calendar file (Lotus Organizer)
OR2 Calendar file (Lotus Organizer 2)
OR3 Lotus Organizer 97 file

P

PBM Portable bitmap graphic
PCM Audio file
PCW Text file (PC Write)
PCX PC Paintbrush bitmap (ZSoft)
PDF Portable Document file (Adobe Acrobat)
PGP Encrypted file
PKR Public Keyring (PGP)
PM6 Document (PageMaker 6.0)
PNT Graphic file (MacPaint)
PPT PowerPoint presentation (Microsoft)
PUB Publication (Ventura Publisher)
PUB Document (Microsoft Publisher)
PUB Public key ring file (PGP)
PWL Password list file (Microsoft Windows 9.x)

Q

QRY Query (Microsoft)
QT Movie file (QuickTime)
QTI Image file (QuickTime)
QTIF Image file (QuickTime)
QTM Movie file (QuickTime)

R

RAM Metafile (RealAudio)
RAS Bitmap (Sun Raster Images)
REM Remarks file (generic)
RIF RIFF Bitmap graphics (Fractal Design Painter)
RIF Image file (Metacreations Painter 5)
RLE Run-Length Encoded bitmap
RTF Rich Text Format document

S

SAM Document (AMI Professional)

T

TIF Tag image bitmap file (TIFF)
TIFF Tag image bitmap file (TIFF)
TXT ASCII text-formatted audio data

V

VBS Script file (Microsoft Visual Basic)
VOX Audio file (Talking Technology)

W

WK1 Spreadsheet (Lotus 1-2-3 v. 1 and 2)
WK3 Spreadsheet (Lotus 1-2-3 v. 3)
WK4 Spreadsheet (Lotus 1-2-3 v. 4)
WKB Document file (Microsoft WordPerfect for Windows)
WKS Worksheet spreadsheet (Lotus 1-2-3)
WKS Document (Microsoft Works)
WMF Metafile (Microsoft Windows)
WP Document file (Microsoft WordPerfect for Windows)
WPA Word processor document
WP4 Document (Microsoft WordPerfect for Windows 4.0)
WP5 Document (Microsoft WordPerfect for Windows 5.0)
WP6 Document (Microsoft WordPerfect for Windows 6.0
WPS Text document (Microsoft Works)
WRI Write document (Windows Write)
WS7 Document (WordStar for Windows version 7)
WSD Document (WordStar for Windows 2000)

X

XLB Datafile (Microsoft Excel)
XLC Chart file (Microsoft Excel)
XML eXtensible markup language
XLS Spreadsheet (Microsoft Excel)

Z

ZIP Zip file Compressed archive

No one book can answer all questions, so it is very possible you will be faced with challenges that require more information. This is especially true if you are having a problem with a particular make of component (soundcard, graphics card or modem). Knowing where to go for help is as important as finding the solution. It often boils down to asking the right question in the right place.

There are three key sources of information: the Internet, magazines and books, and knowledgeable friends.

The Internet

Without doubt, the Internet is an amazing source of information on everything to do with computers and information technology. But – and this is a big 'but' – finding what you really want is often a real challenge. It has always been true, even before the advent of the Worldwide Web, that online searching requires some practice. The real truth of this is demonstrated in the graphic below, which shows the results of a Google search about searching. Look both in the box next to the large 'Google' for the query and below to see that there were over 700,000 results! Fortunately, most search engines put the best results at the beginning. It is always worth looking through the first 10–15 results.

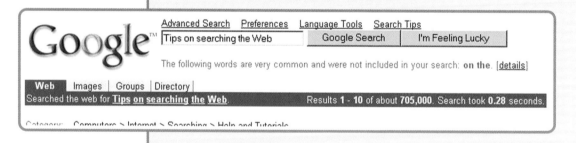

Several websites offer good advice on searching the Internet. One useful one is http://searchenginewatch.com, which helpfully divides its resources into topics designed to improve your searching technique.

There are many search engines (at least 800), and using more than two or three may seem a daunting task. Spend a useful ten minutes exploring Phil Bradley's home page at www.philb.com for some great keys to many of the Internet's doors to knowledge. Also, by using a tool which combines the activities of several search engines at once, you can maximise your chances of getting a good result. (You could, of course, also end up being overwhelmed by the results.) A good tool for this approach is Copernic. Go to www.copernic.com to try its free, basic search tool.

Magazine and books

Just spending 15 minutes in a bookshop or at a newsagent's browsing the computer magazines will demonstrate that many useful sources on help and advice are to be found. Computer magazines cover all areas of interest, and range from those aimed at the IT professional to those suitable for a complete novice. Very many computer magazines have cover CD-ROMs which are stuffed full of useful utilities, shareware, game demos and a host of programs covering everything from home accounting to desktop publishing. It is worth trying a different magazine each month for a few months rather than buying lots at the same time.

Books about computers, computing and information technology abound, at every level, from complete beginner to dyed-in-the-wool geek. Look at purchasers' reviews of a title you are interested in on any of the online book suppliers. Many magazines too publish book reviews and these should be consulted before you go out and spend £15-£30 on a book.

Knowledgeable friends

You probably know somebody who can help. Friends and neighbours who already use PCs may well have experienced the problems you are facing and found a solution. Ask! Such advice is likely to be free and, because it is often based on practical experience, very useful. A word of caution is necessary. You need to feel comfortable that your friend or neighbour really does know enough about the subject, otherwise it might be more effective to go back to your supplier or ring a help-line.

Another source of information

A fourth source of information, used commonly before the Net became popular, is Usenet. Commonly referred to as newsgroups (see section 7.8), they exist on most topics. There are masses of them about computing, both software and hardware. You will find newsgroups devoted to all of Microsoft's products, and specific groups for a variety of hardware such as printers. Equipment such printers and scanners are commonly found in newsgroups like these.

alt.binaries.printers.utilities
alt.crimehip.laser-printers
alt.emircpih.laser-printers
alt.h.i.p.c.r.i.m.e.laser-printers
alt.h1pcr1me.laser-printers
alt.hh.ii.pp.cc.rr.ii.mm.ee.laser-printers
alt.hipclone.laser-printers
alt.hipcrime.laser-printers
comp.laser-printers
comp.periphs.printers

The Internet has thousands of sites useful to you as a PC user. The listings that follow are merely a few suggestions. Always remember, website addresses come and go as sites change and develop. All these links were working at the time of writing.

SEARCHING FOR ADVICE

One of the best ways to find specific information on the Internet is to use a search engine. A very popular (and good) one is www.google.com. You can type phrases into the search box, such as 'What's a good graphics card', and find thousands of responses. The results are listed in order of the most matching sites. Usually the first 10-15 results will provide some useful material. As always, in order to find an answer, you have to know the correct question. Trial and error works very well, and learning some of the tricks of searching pays dividends. All the search engines offer clear advice on searching techniques.

BUYING GUIDES AND PRODUCT REVIEWS

www.bestpricecomputers.ltd.uk/ guides/

www.zdnet.co.uk

www.amazon.co.uk
Go to the Software tab and then select Buying Guides

www.one2surf.co.uk/enduser/ buyingzone/guides.asp

www.dealtime.co.uk

http://gamespot.com

www.gamesdomain.co.uk/

www.hardwarecentral.com

www.itreviews.co.uk

www.sharkyextreme.com

IT SUPPORT, ADVICE AND NEWS

www.cnet.com
This is a very useful site for all sorts of IT stuff and an enormous source of shareware downloads for PC users

www.techrepublic.com
Another plentiful source of information. You have to subscribe, but it is free

www.annoyances.org/
A wonderful source of down-to-earth information for PC users

www.idg.net/

www.wired.com

CONSUMER ADVICE

www.tradingstandards.gov.uk/
Useful government site covering current standards

www.trustuk.org.uk/
Government-backed, non-profit-making scheme to help online consumers by regulating Internet codes of practice

PC COMPONENT AND PERIPHERAL MANUFACTURERS

These suppliers may have a UK site under the .co.uk suffix

www.seagate.com

www.maxtor.com

www.wdc.com

www.storage.ibm.com

www.fcpa.com/

www.epson.com

www.hp.com

www.canon.co.uk/

www.oki.co.uk

www.printgrc.com/drivers. cfm#manufacturers
This site has a very useful list of all printer manufacturers' websites

www.amd.com
Processor manufacturers

www.intel.com
Processor manufacturers

ANTI-VIRUS SOFTWARE VENDORS

http://antivirus.about.com/cs/ antivirusvendors/index.htm
This site gives a useful list of most anti-virus vendors

www.grisoft.com/
This site is not listed in the link above, but is the source of AVG – a good and free package

HARDWARE, TIPS AND TROUBLESHOOTING

www.tomshardware.com
A key site for information about PC hardware, especially motherboards

www.motherboards.org/
Another highly informative site about motherboards

www.cdfreaks.com
A great site for help in using CDs and CD-ROM drives

www.driverguide.com
One of the best sites for drivers. You need to subscribe, but it is free

www.troubleshooters.com
An interesting, but useful, amateur site

www.microsoft.com/windowsxp/ home/default.asp
Windows XP Home Edition

SAFE INTERNET USE FOR YOUNG PEOPLE

www.msn.staysafeonline.com/

www.safekids.com/safeteens/

www.kidsmart.org.uk/

www.chatdanger.com/

www.getnetwise.org/

www.microsoft.com/privacy/ safeinternet/topics/children.htm

Index

Which? Books are commissioned and researched by
Consumers' Association and published by
Which? Ltd, 2 Marylebone Road, London NW1 4DF
Email address: books@which.net

Distributed by The Penguin Group:
Penguin Books Ltd, 80 Strand, London WC2R 0RL

Design: Paul Sands
Technical consultants: Roy Brooker, Fraser Henderson
Editorial and production: Joanna Bregosz, Nithya Rae

The publishers would like to thank Will Garside, Jason Harris, Joe McAllister, Simon Rowley and Richard Wentk for their
assistance with the first edition.

First edition October 2000
Reprinted 2001
Second edition May 2002
Copyright © 2002 Which? Ltd

British Library Cataloguing in Publication Data
A catalogue record for this book is available from the British Library

ISBN 0 85202 881 4

For a full list of Which? books, please write to Which? Books, Castlemead,
Gascoyne Way, Hertford X, SG14 1LH or access our website at www.which.net

Cover design by Sarah Harmer

Free trial to Computing Which?
For more help on getting the most from your computer, take out a free trial of **Computing Which?**.

This bi-monthly magazine is packed with reviews of the best and worst digital cameras, printers, scanners, software,
and more. It also has practical step-by-step guides to using your computer — how to set up a website, for instance,
as well as using advanced word-processor features, editing camcorder films, or producing a newsletter. There are
also regular website reviews, the latest computer news, solutions to readers' problems, and investigations of
computer rip-offs. **Computing Which?** is available by subscription only. For a free trial, Freephone 0800 252100
(payment details required for when free trial ends).

Text reproduction by Saxon Photolitho, Norwich
Printed and bound in Spain by Bookprint, Barcelona